RANGE RIDERS COOKIN'

Created by:

BOB KERBY'S
LONGHORN STUDIO

415 46th Ave. • Kearney, NE 68845

Phone: (308) 236-6379

www.ExperienceTheWest.com

ISBN 13 978-0-9660523-0-5
ISBN 0-9660523-0-7

Printed in the United States of America.

Welcome to the Western

First pony age 8 Colorado Springs, Colorado.

Robert E. Kerby has devoted a lifetime capturing the action of the American West and the life of the modern day cowboy. Reared in Colorado he left home at age 17 to work on large cattle ranches in northern New Mexico.

Bronc riding in Trinidad, Colorado 1950.

Living the life of a cowboy sparked Kerby's romance for the west and the necesary knowledge to create authentic artwork.

World of Bob Kerby!

Roping in Denver, Colorado 71st birthday June 2000.

Kerby paints exclusively in oils and has exhibited in western art shows throughout the United States. His paintings hang in public and private collections from New York to Australia. Kerby's work has been featured on magazine covers, and reproduced in the form of post cards, Christmas cards, posters, limited edition collector prints, cookbooks and calendars. It is estimated that over 4 million people a year view his famous Range Riders appointment calendar.

Bob on his good colt Rusty - Kerby Ranch.

Bob's love for horses, the West and the cowboy way of life can be shared and enjoyed by visiting:

www.ExperienceTheWest.com

FOREWORD

We all enjoy good DOWN HOME cookin' and **RANGE RIDERS COOKIN'** features a special and unique collection of mouthwaterin recipes providing you with enjoyable moments of fun and ease in preparing and feasting on a wide variety of delicious dishes! From the old-time favorites Grandma whipped up to the exquisite dishes prepared by today's top professional chefs, **RANGE RIDERS COOKIN'** is a pleasurable experience in cooking.

You will also treasure the breathtaking western artwork featured throughout this publication by nationally recognized artist Robert E. Kerby. Kerby captures in painstaking detail the true spirit of the American West. The western way of life is a part of our American heritage, and we are delighted to share with you these classic recipes and quality western artwork.

Robert E Kerby

RANGE RIDERS COOKIN' gives new meaning to the saying:

Home on the "Range"

So... Good Luck, Dig In, & Happy Cookin'!

TABLE OF CONTENTS

CABIN CREEK CHEESE BALL

Grind and mix well:

1 pkg. (8-oz.) cream cheese
1/2 lb. American cheese

1/2 lb. sharp cheddar cheese
1/2 lb. Velveeta cheese

Add, to taste:

Garlic powder

Worcestershire sauce

Make into a roll or ball and roll in 1 cup finely-chopped pecans. Sprinkle with paprika. (Optional:) Add Tabasco to taste. Serve with crackers.

TRAILSIDE CHEESE BALL

3/4 c. grated cheddar cheese
2 green onions, diced
1 pkg. dried beef, chopped

1 (8-oz.) pkg. cream cheese, softened
Chopped walnuts

Mix together all ingredients but walnuts, adding cream cheese last. Roll into a ball and then roll in chopped walnuts. Serve with crackers.

X-COUNTRY SARDINE SPREAD

2 sm. cans sardines, with oil
2 hard-boiled eggs, finely-chopped

Juice from 1/2 lemon
1/4 tsp. dill weed
Rye crackers

In a small mixing bowl combine all the ingredients and blend thoroughly. Pack in covered container. Great snack for spreading on crackers.

TEXAS TEASERS

Remove crusts from 1 loaf (1 pound) sandwich bread. Cut slices into 4 triangles and toast on both sides. Spread with mixture of:

2 bunches green onions, chopped (tops also)
1 lb. bacon, cooked & crumbled

3/4 c. mayonnaise
Dash of pepper

Use about 1 teaspoon mixture on each triangle. Yields 5 dozen.

MISS KITTY'S GARDEN VEGETABLE DIP

16 oz. sour cream
1 container plain yogurt
1 env. Hidden Valley Original
  Ranch dressing mix

1/2 jar Marie's avocado dressing
or 1 container avocado chip
dip

Blend together.

MULESKINNER'S CHIPPED BEEF DIP

Soften 2 packages (8-ounce each) cream cheese. Add 2 bunches green onions (chopped very fine; tops also) and 1 jar dried chipped beef. Chill.

CHESTER'S CHEESE AND BACON DIP

1 pkg. Velveeta cheese
6 crispy-fried bacon slices
4 chopped green onions

Garlic salt
Pepper, opt.

In a saucepan melt cheese over low heat. Add garlic salt and stir constantly. Crumble crispy-fried bacon slices. Add along with green onions to cheese mixture. Serve warm with chips of your choice.

BANDITS BEAN DIP

1 (16-oz.) can Rosarita refried
  beans
1 (3-oz.) pkg. cream cheese
2 T. grated onion or 1/2 tsp.
  onion powder

1 tsp. chili pepper
1/4 tsp. garlic powder
1 tsp. salt

Soften cream cheese. Blend in remaining ingredients. Mix well and chill. Serve with crisp Rosarita corn tortillas.

CALAMITY JANE'S TACO SALAD DIP

3 med. ripe avocados
2 T. lemon juice
1/2 tsp. salt
1/4 tsp. pepper
1 c. sour cream
1/2 c. mayonnaise
1 pkg. (1/4-1 1/8-oz.) taco
  seasoning mix
2 (10 1/2-oz.) cans jalapeno bean
  dip

1 lg. bunch green onions
3 med. tomatoes (cored,
  seeded, & coarsely chopped)
2 (3 1/2-oz.) cans ripe black olives
1 (8-oz.) pkg. sharp cheddar
  cheese, shredded
1 lg. pkg. tortilla chips

Peel and pit and mash avocados; add lemon juice, salt, and pepper. Combine sour cream, mayonnaise, and taco seasoning mix. Layer bottom with bean dip; top with avocado mixture. Layer with sour cream and taco mix. Sprinkle with onions, tomato, and olives. Cover with shredded cheese. Serve with tortilla chips.

RANCHERO NACHO DIP

1 lb. Owen's country sausage (mild)
16 oz. Velveeta cheese

2 cans tomatoes & chili greens

Fry off sausage; drain. Melt cheese. Partially drain tomatoes and chili greens. Add to melted cheese. Add sausage. Serve warm on plain nachos. For milder version, use just one can tomatoes and chili greens.

GUACAMOLE DIP

2 med. avocados, ripe
1 T. lemon juice
2 med. tomatoes, peeled, finely chopped

1 c. onions, finely chopped
1 tsp. seasoned salt
1/4 tsp. seasoned pepper

Mash the peeled avocados with a fork. Add the lemon juice and blend. Add the remaining ingredients and combine thoroughly. Serve with chips.

COVERED WAGON DIP

Brown and drain 1 cup pecan pieces and 2 tablespoons butter. Set aside. Heat:

16 oz. cream cheese
1/4 c. milk
2 cans (4-oz.) chipped beef
1/2 tsp. garlic salt

4 tsp. minced onion
1 c. sour cream
1 c. chopped chilies

Mix well. Sprinkle with the pecans. Bake in a preheated 350° oven for about 20 minutes, or until heated through. Serve warm with crackers.

BUCKAROO BARBECUED CHICKEN WINGS

3/4 c. chili sauce
1/2 c. cola-flavored soda

1/2 tsp. onion salt
3 lbs. (about 16) chicken wings

Combine chili sauce, soda, and onion salt in bowl. Cover and refrigerate. Cut off wing tips and reserve for soup, if you wish. Slicing through the joint, cut each wing in half. Cover and refrigerate. **To grill:** Cook chicken 4 inches from gray coals (medium heat), turning often with tongs. Cook 20 minutes. Remove chicken from grill. Dip chicken in sauce and return to grill. Cook 10 minutes more, turning often, until well glazed. Makes about 32 appetizers.

TENDERFOOT CHICKEN TIDBITS

2 whole chicken breasts
1/4 c. butter
2 tsp. Dijon mustard
1 clove garlic, crushed
1 T. chopped parsley

1 tsp. lemon juice
1/8 tsp. salt
1/4 c. fine dry bread crumbs
1/4 c. Parmesan cheese

Skin and bone chicken breasts. Cut into 3/4-inch cubes. Melt butter in skillet and add mustard, garlic, parsley, lemon juice, and salt. Brown chicken on all sides. In a paper sack add bread crumbs and Parmesan cheese. Add chicken and shake to coat evenly. Serve either warm or cold with toothpicks.

BAT MASTERSON MEATBALLS

1 env. beefy onion soup mix
1 1/2 lbs. ground beef
1/2 c. soft bread crumbs
1 egg
2 T. brown sugar
1 1/2 T. cornstarch
1 can (20-oz.) pineapple chunks in natural juice, drained (reserve juice)

1/4 c. vinegar
1/4 c. water
2 green peppers, cut into chunks

In medium bowl, combine beefy onion soup mix, ground beef, bread crumbs, and egg. Shape into 1-inch meatballs. In 3-quart casserole blend sugar, cornstarch, reserved juice, vinegar and water; add green pepper. Heat, covered, stirring occasionally 8 minutes or until meatballs are done. Makes about 5 dozen meatballs. **Conventional directions:** Prepare meatballs as above. In large skillet, brown meatballs; remove to serving dish and keep warm. Into skillet, add brown sugar and cornstarch blended with reserved juice, vinegar, and water. Stir in pineapple and green pepper. Bring to a boil, then simmer, stirring constantly, until sauce is thickened, about 5 minutes. Serve over meatballs.

TEXAS TRASH

Mix and stir constantly until it boils:

1 c. butter
2 T. Lawry's seasoned salt
2 T. garlic

2 T. Tabasco sauce
2 T. Worcestershire sauce

Set aside and mix in large mixing bowl:

1 box Wheat Chex
1 box Cheerios

2 lbs. nuts
1 box Rice Chex

Stir all together until cereal is moist. Bake in long pan, stirring occasionally at 250° for 1 hour.

KICKAPOO PUNCH

1 (6-oz.) can frozen lemonade
1 (6-oz.) can frozen orange juice
1 (6-oz.) can grape juice
1 (46-oz.) can red Hawaiian
  punch

6 c. cold water
1 pt. 12-oz. bottle ginger ale

Mix lemonade, orange juice, grape juice, and punch. Add 6 cups cold water. Just before serving, add chilled ginger ale. Makes 30-35 servings.

TIN CUP PUNCH

1 (12-oz.) can frozen fruit punch
1 qt. lemon lime soda
1 lemon, sliced
Cherries

3 cans water
1 orange, sliced
1 tangerine, sliced

Mix all ingredients except the soda and chill thoroughly. Add soda just before serving. You can use an ice block made in a Jello mold to keep punch cold while setting out.

RIVER CITY FRUIT PUNCH

3 qts. unsweetened pineapple
  juice
Juice of 8 lemons OR 1¹/₂ c.
  juice
Juice of 8 oranges OR 2 c. juice
Juice of 3 limes OR ¹/₂ c. juice
2 c. sugar
1 c. mint leaves
4 qts. dry ginger ale
1 qt. plain soda water
1 pt. strawberries, quartered OR
  1 pkg. frozen

Combine fruit juices, sugar, and mint leaves; chill thoroughly. Just before serving, add ginger ale, soda water, and strawberries. Pour over large cake of ice in punch bowl. Float thin slices of lemon, lime, or orange. Serves 35. **Note:** Base may be frozen ahead.

PRESCOTT PARTY PUNCH

1 (46-oz.) can pineapple juice
1 qt. cranberry juice cocktail
3 (28-oz.) bottles ginger ale
¹/₂ c. lemon juice
6 orange slices

Have all ingredients chilled. Pour over ice in punch bowl. Garnish with orange slices. Makes about 25 cups.

TRAIL DRIVER'S TEA COOLER

3 tea bags or 1 T. loose black
  tea
1¹/₂ c. boiling water
¹/₂ c. fresh lemon juice
1 bottle (28-oz.) lemon lime
  carbonated beverage, or
  ginger ale, chilled
³/₄-1 c. sugar
1 tray ice cubes
¹/₂ c. fresh orange juice

Place tea bags or loose tea in bowl. Pour boiling water over tea. Let stand 5 minutes. Remove bags or strain to remove leaves. Add sugar and stir until all is dissolved. Place ice cubes in 2-quart serving pitcher. Pour hot tea, lemon, and orange juice over tea. Stir briskly several seconds until mixture is cold. Stir in chilled lemon-lime carbonated beverage. Pour into glasses and serve at once. (Makes 2 quarts.)

OGALLALA TEA AND TANG MIX

1 c. instant tea
1 c. Tang
1¹/₂ c. sugar
¹/₂ tsp. cinnamon
¹/₂ tsp. cloves

Mix and store in an airtight container in a dry place. To serve, place 2 heaping teaspoonfuls in a cup. Fill with hot water. **Optional:** Add red hot cinnamon candy.

CANON CITY APPLE CIDER

Mix in large pan:

1/2 gal. apple cider	1 1/2 c. sugar
Juice of 3 or 4 lemons	2 c. water

Mix together in 6-inch square piece of cloth; tie with a st drop into liquid the following:

2 tsp. cinnamon	1 T. cloves
1 tsp. allspice	2 tsp. pickling spices

Boil several minutes. Then turn on very low heat to just keep hot. (This will smell so good through the entire house.) Serve in mugs while hot.

LOGGER LOVER HOT SPICED PUNCH

For 30-cup percolator:

9 c. unsweetened pineapple juice	1/2 c. brown sugar
9 c. cranberry juice cocktail	4 tsp. whole cloves
4 1/4 c. water	4 cinnamon sticks, broken
	1/4 tsp. salt

For 10-cup percolator:

3 c. unsweetened pineapple juice	1/4 c. brown sugar
3 c. cranberry juice cocktail	1 1/2 tsp. whole cloves
1 1/2 c. water	1 cinnamon stick, broken
	1/8 tsp. salt

Combine first 3 ingredients in automatic percolator. Combine remaining ingredients in basket. Allow to go through the perk cycle.

MISSOULA HOT CHOCOLATE MIX

Blend well:

6 c. powdered milk	1 c. cocoa
1 1/2 c. sugar	1/4 tsp. salt

Store in airtight container in dry place. For each serving, place 4 tablespoons of mix in each cup. Fill with boiling water. (Top with whipped cream and a dash of ground cinnamon.)

Robert E. Kerby
B/K

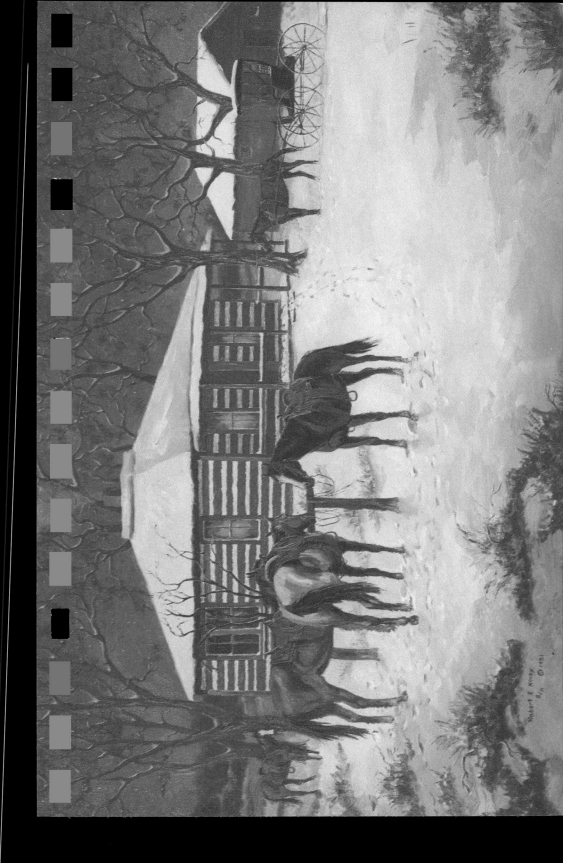

SIX SHOOTER STEAK SOUP

1/2 c. oleo	1 c. celery
1 c. flour	2 c. frozen mixed vegetables
1/2 gal. water	1 can tomatoes
3 c. stew meat	1 T. Accent
1 c. onions	2 T. beef bouillon
1 c. carrots	1 T. black pepper

Melt oleo and whip in 1 cup flour to make smooth paste. Stir in 1/2 gallon water. Heat and stir until slightly thickened. Saute stew meat. Add beef to soup. Add onion, carrots, and celery, which have been parboiled. Add 2 cups frozen mixed vegetables, 1 can tomatoes, and 1 teaspoon seasonings. Simmer until vegetables are done. Freezes well.

OLD SETTLER'S HAMBURGER SOUP

Brown 1 pound hamburger in 2 tablespoons butter. Add 1 quart boiling water and 2 tablespoons beef bouillon. Then add 1 (#303) can tomatoes, 2 cups sliced carrots, 1 cup diced celery, and 1/3 cup (regular) round barley. Simmer 1-1 1/2 hours. If desired, add 2 cups diced potatoes during last 1/2 hour of cooking.

CHUCKHOLE CHARLIE'S CHICKEN SOUP

1 soup chicken (4 lbs.)	2 sprigs parsley
2 qts. water	2 sprigs dill
1 whole onion	2 tsp. salt
2 whole carrots	1/4 tsp. pepper
4 stalks celery, incl. tops	2 tsp. sugar
1 parsnip root, cleaned	

Place chicken in deep pot; add water and remaining ingredients except sugar. Bring to boil; simmer covered, until chicken is tender, about 2 hours. Remove chicken. Strain soup and chill. Skim off fat which has risen to the top of chilled soup. Reheat soup. Add sugar. Serve with a piece of carrot and chicken, matzo, or noodle in each bowl.

PAWNEE POTATO SOUP

4 slices bacon, finely chopped	4 c. water
1/4 onion, finely chopped	1 egg
4 med. potatoes, diced	Salt, pepper
Flour	

Brown bacon and onion. Add water and potatoes. Cook until tender. Make a soft noodle dough with egg and flour. Roll out and cut off in strips and add to potatoes. Cook until done. A little thickening may be used if you wish.

MID-WESTERN CHOWDER

3 c. diced potatoes	1/2 c. margarine
1/2 c. sliced carrots	1/2 c. flour
1/2 c. sliced celery	3 c. milk
1/4 c. chopped onion	1 (4-oz.) pkg. Cracker Barrel
1 1/2 tsp. pepper	cheese, shredded
2 c. water	2 c. corn (may be cream-style)

Combine potatoes, carrots, celery, onion, salt, and pepper. Add water; cover and simmer 10 minutes. Do not drain. Make a cream sauce with margarine, flour, and milk. Add cheese and stir until melted. Add corn and undrained vegetables. Heat; do not boil.

BADLANDS VEGETABLE SOUP

2 lbs. round steak, trim & cut into 1-inch cubes	3 stalks celery, sliced in 2-inch strips
1 (16-oz.) can whole tomatoes	3 lg. carrots, cut into 2-inch strips
1/2 head shredded cabbage	2 c. water
1 med. onion, sliced thin	

Brown meat, including bone into 2 tablespoons butter or margarine. Put into a 3-quart stock pot and add water, tomatoes (mashed) and onion. Bring to a boil; turn down the heat to simmer for 1 1/2 hours, stirring occasionally. After 1 1/2 hours, add cabbage, carrots, and celery. Simmer another 45 minutes, adding more water if needed. Add salt and pepper to taste.

SALLY'S SWISS POTATO SOUP

6 thick slices bacon, cut into
 1/2-inch pieces
2 lg. leeks, thinly sliced
2 c. minced onion
3 med. potatoes, pared & cubed

1 lg. turnip, pared & cubed
6 c. chicken broth
1 c. sour cream
Dried dill weed

Fry bacon until crisp in Dutch oven; remove bacon. Add leeks and onions to hot fat. Saute, covered, until tender (10 minutes). Add potatoes, turnips, and broth. Heat to boiling; reduce heat. Simmer, covered, until vegetables are tender, about 15 minutes. Puree mixture in blender. Return puree to Dutch oven. Heat to boil; stir in sour cream with whisk. To serve, add bits of bacon and dash of dill to each bowl.

JANE'S COWBOY BEAN SOUP

1 lb. dried white pea beans
3 qts. water
1/4 lb. smoked bacon, diced
1 lg. onion, chopped
1 carrot, chopped
2 c. chopped celery
1/2 sm. green pepper, chopped
1 1/2 cloves minced garlic

3 qts. water
1/2 lb. diced ham
1/2 tsp. Tabasco sauce
1 tsp. seasoning salt
1/2 c. catsup
1 T. sugar
1 T. finely-chopped parsley
1/2 tsp. paprika

Cover beans with water and soak overnight. Drain. Saute smoked bacon over low heat for 5 minutes. Add vegetables to bacon and cook over low heat until vegetables are wilted. Add 3 quarts of water, the drained beans, ham, Tabasco sauce, seasoning salt, catsup, sugar, parsley, and paprika. Bring all ingredients to a boil and simmer, covered, 2 1/2-3 hours, until beans are tender. Serve immediately or refrigerate overnight and reheat the following day. Makes 8 servings.

OLD CHAPS ONION SOUP

2 T. oil or margarine
1 1/2 c. onions, thinly sliced
6 c. beef broth

Black pepper
Parmesan cheese
6 slices French bread, toasted

Saute onions in oil until transparent and thoroughly cooked. Add broth and black pepper. Simmer 30 minutes. Divide into 6 oven-proof casseroles or bowls. Top each with a slice of toasted French bread. Sprinkle with Parmesan cheese. Place in broiler until cheese is melted. Serve immediately. Yields 1 1/2 quarts.

SODBUSTER PEA SOUP

1½ lbs. smoked ham shank	2 tsp. crushed marjoram
3 c. split peas	Pepper to taste
1 c. lentils	Onion powder to taste
7 c. water	

Put peas and lentils in kettle. Add water, ham, and seasonings. Bring to a boil, then cover and simmer 1 hour or until peas are tender. Serves 14-16.

BUCKAROO BEAN SOUP

Soak overnight in water:

1 c. dried Great Northern beans or tiny white beans	1 tsp. cooking oil
	1 tsp. salt

Drain and add:

4 c. water

Chop and add:

1 c. ham	1 med. onion
2 stalks celery	3 carrots
½ c. green peppers	

Then add:

1 can tomato puree	1 tsp. mustard
1 tsp. sugar	1 whole clove

Add to taste:

Salt & pepper

Cook in a pressure cooker for about 20 minutes. Remove lid and boil a few minutes to let juice thicken. Can also be cooked slow, covered, until beans are soft and done. Add a pan of hot cornbread and have a hearty meal. Yields 8 servings.

COWGIRL SALAD

1 can (16-oz.) pitted Bing
  cherries, drain & reserve juice
1 can (16-oz.) crushed
  pineapple, drain & reserve
  juice

Add enough water to the juice to make 1½ cups. Bring to a boil and add 1 package (6-ounce) cherry Jello. Dissolve well and add 2 cups Coca-Cola, 1 cup chopped nuts, and drained pineapple and cherries. Pour into serving dish and congeal.

WESTERN KANSAS 7-UP SALAD

Bring to a boil 2 cups water. Add 1 package (6-ounce) lemon Jello. Dissolve well and add:

2 c. 7-Up
1 c. miniature marshmallows
2 bananas, sliced

1 can (20-oz.) crushed pineapple
   (drain & save juice)

Put in refrigerator to congeal. Combine and cook until thick:

2 T. butter
1/2 c. sugar
2 T. flour

1 c. pineapple juice
1 egg

When thickened, remove from heat and let cool completely. Add 1 cup whipped topping and spread over Jello. Sprinkle with grated cheese. Yields 10 servings.

STRAWBERRY ROANIE'S JELLO

Mix together:

1 box (6-oz.) strawberry Jello,
   dry

1 can (#2) crushed pineapple
1 lg. carton Cool Whip

Fold in:

1 c. small curd cottage cheese

Chill and serve.

RUSTY'S RHUBARB SALAD

Use 2 cups cooked rhubarb, with sugar. While rhubarb is hot, stir in one package of cherry Jello. Let congeal, then add 1 medium can crushed pineapple (drained) and 1/2 cup nutmeats.

PISTOL PACKIN PETE'S PISTACHIO DELIGHT

1-lb. box or 2 sm. boxes
   sugar-free pistachio pudding
1 lg. can crushed pineapple,
   drained
1/2 c. chopped pecans
1 c. chopped red apple,
   unpeeled

1 c. flaked or shredded coconut
1 (16-oz.) bag miniature
   marshmallows
1 (8-oz.) carton Cool Whip
1/3 c. chopped maraschino
   cherries

Mix all ingredients together and refrigerate until ready to serve. Serves 12-15.

BRONC BUSTERS "WHOA BOY" FRUIT SALAD

Mix all together, including juice:

1 lg. can fruit cocktail
1 med. can chunked pineapple
1 c. chopped pecans
4 bananas, cut in large chunks

1½ pkgs. French vanilla or vanilla instant pudding & pie filling, dry

Chill and serve.

PALOMINO LEMON COCONUT SURPRISE

2 c. sour cream
1 pkg. (4-serving size) Jello lemon instant pudding & pie filling

1⅓ c. (about) Baker's Angel Flake coconut
1 can (8¼-oz.) crushed pineapple in syrup

Combine sour cream and pudding mix. Add coconut and pineapple. Stir until blended. Serve at once or chill in serving dish.

SUNDOWNER APPLE NUT SALAD

3 med. green apples
1 c. chopped English walnuts
3 med. red apples
1 c. mayonnaise

1½ c. celery
Lettuce leaves
1½ c. raisins

Core and dice the apples, but do not peel. Add celery, raisins, and chopped walnuts and mix well. Add mayonnaise and toss until mayonnaise is evenly mixed.

BATTLE MOUNTAIN MANDARIN ORANGE SALAD

Drain and reserve liquid from 3 cans mandarin orange segments. Heat the juice with enough water to total 3 cups liquid. Dissolve in the hot liquid 1 package (6-ounce) orange-flavored Jello. Cool. Combine with the mandarin oranges 2 cans water chestnuts (drained and sliced paper thin). Chill until firm. Combine 1 package (3-ounce) cream cheese (softened), ½ cup chopped fresh orange sections, and ½ cup chopped crystallized ginger. Add ¼ cup cream. Spread the dressing over the congealed salad. Dressing should be consistency of mayonnaise, so add, or take from, the cream. Yields 10-12 servings.

DANCE HALL FRUIT SALAD

Thaw 1 package (10-ounce) frozen strawberries. Add 1/2 cup sugar. Drain and add 1 can (8-ounce) pineapple chunks and 1 can apricot pie filling. Slice and add 2 bananas. Mix together and chill overnight. Yields 10-12 servings.

CABIN CREEK CRANBERRY SALAD

1 lb. raw cranberries, ground
3 ground apples
1 1/2 c. sugar
2 (3-oz.) pkgs. raspberry Jello

3 c. hot water
1/2 lb. miniature marshmallows
1 (9-oz.) carton Cool Whip

Mix together cranberries, apples, and sugar. Combine Jello and hot water. When Jello is partially set, add the cranberry mixture, marshmallows, and Cool Whip. Chill until firm. Serves 15.

COWHAND'S CHRISTMAS SALAD

Grind 1 cup cranberries and 1 orange (quarter and remove seeds; grind rind also). Cook a few minutes with 1 cup sugar. Set aside. Dissolve 1 (3-ounce) package strawberry Jello in 1 cup boiling water. Add to above mixture. Stir in 1 cup pineapple juice, 1 cup pineapple tidbits, and 1/2 cup chopped nuts. Pour into a Christmas mold and congeal. Unmold onto a serving plate covered with lettuce leaves. Garnish with mayonnaise. Keep chilled until serving time. Best to make a day ahead. Yields 10 servings.

CATTLE KATE'S CREAMY CABBAGE SLAW

Shred fine and mix together:

1 med. head cabbage
2 carrots
1/2 onion (or 1/4 c. sliced green
   onion)

1 green pepper

Mix in separate bowl and stir until sugar is dissolved:

1 c. mayonnaise or salad
   dressing
2 T. sugar

2 T. vinegar
2 tsp. celery seed
1 tsp. salt

Drizzle over cabbage mixture and toss lightly to mix. Yields 8-10 servings.

COWBOY CLYDE'S CABBAGE SALAD

Combine:

1/2 head red cabbage, shredded
1/2 head white cabbage,
   shredded

Add:

2 red onions, sliced thin	1 c. sliced celery
1 c. grated carrots	1 green pepper, sliced thin

Make a dressing of:

1 c. oil	1 c. white vinegar
1 tsp. salt	1 tsp. dry mustard
1 c. sugar	1 tsp. celery seed

Heat the dressing mixture. Pour over the vegetables while hot. Cover and refrigerate. Let set for 24 hours in refrigerator before serving. Will keep several days.

OK CORRAL CAULIFLOWER SALAD

**Clean and chop to the size you
   prefer:**

1 head cauliflower	Celery
1 green pepper	

Add cubed cheddar cheese. Cover with Hidden Valley Ranch dressing. Cover and store in refrigerator until ready to use. Toss and serve.

CODY CARROT SALAD

Combine:

2 c. shredded carrots
1 can (20-oz.) pineapple tidbits,
   drained

Cover and refrigerate overnight. When ready to serve, add:

1 c. coconut	1 c. miniature marshmallows

Toss and cover with a dressing of:

3 oz. cream cheese, softened	1/2 c. whipped topping
1/2 c. mayonnaise	

WESTERN VEGETABLE SALAD

1/2 c. oil
1/4 c. lemon juice
2 tsp. sugar
1 tsp. salt
1/2 tsp. ground cumin
1 clove garlic, crushed
6 lg. tomatoes

2 cucumbers, peeled & thinly
  sliced
2/3 c. onion, minced
1 green pepper, diced
1 c. (3 7/8-oz.) can pitted ripe
  olives

Prepare dressing by blending together oil, lemon juice, sugar, salt, and cumin. Spear garlic on wood picks and put in dressing. Let dressing stand at least 2 hours before mixing with salad. Remove garlic. Makes 3/4 cup. An hour before serving, cut tomatoes in 3/4-inch chunks. Mix with remaining salad ingredients in large salad bowl. Add enough dressing so vegetables are moist. Marinate for 1 hour. Serves 8-10.

HIGH MESA MARINATED VEGETABLE SALAD

1 (#2) can corn, drained
1 (#2) can French-style green
  beans, drained
1 (#2) can peas and carrots,
  drained

1 sm. jar pimentos
1 c. chopped celery
1 onion, chopped
Salt & pepper

Dressing:

1/2 c. vegetable oil
1 1/2 c. sugar

1 c. vinegar

Add celery and onion to drained vegetables. Salt and pepper to taste. Combine sugar, vinegar, and oil and pour over vegetables. Refrigerate at least 24 hours before serving. Stir several times. Keeps 2-3 weeks.

TOM MIX MARINATED MUSHROOMS

1 pkg. Good Seasons Italian
  salad dressing

1 pkg. Good Seasons garlic
  salad dressing

Mix as directed on package, then add and mix:

1/4 c. chopped onion
1/4 c. green pepper, chopped
4-6 (4-oz.) jars mushrooms
  (Green Giant)

1 (4-oz.) jar pimentos

Drain mushrooms and pimentos. Chill overnight.

HOP SING'S VEGETABLE SALAD

Combine:

1 can French-cut green beans, drained
1 can bean sprouts or mixed Chinese vegetables, drained

1/2 c. chopped onion
2 T. chopped pimento

Mix and pour over vegetables:

2/3 c. sugar
2/3 c. vinegar

1/2 c. oil
1/2 tsp. salt

Cover and refrigerate overnight. Drain before serving.

MEDICINE BOW MARINATED BEANS

Drain 3 cans green beans. Slice and add 2 purple onions and 1/2 cup ripe olives. Add 2 cups whole cherry tomatoes. Mix and pour over bean mixture 1/2 cup vinegar, 1/2 cup oil, and 1/4 cup sugar. Add to cover 1 bottle Zestee Italian dressing. Refrigerate at least 24 hours or longer.

WHITE-EYED RICE SALAD

1 c. crushed pineapple, drained
1 c. coconut
1 c. mini marshmallows
1 sm. can mandarin orange sections, drained

1 c. cooked rice
1 c. Cool Whip
2 bananas, sliced

Add pineapple to warm rice; cool. Mix with coconut, marsh-mallows, and oranges sections. Fold in Cool Whip and bananas.

MILE HIGH MACARONI SALAD

1 c. mayonnaise
1 T. vinegar
1 T. prepared mustard
1 tsp. sugar
1 tsp. salt
1/4 tsp. pepper

8-oz. pkg. macaroni, cooked
1 c. sliced celery
1 c. chopped green or sweet red pepper or combination
1/4 c. chopped onion

Optional:

Drained tuna fish
Drained shrimp

Drained crab
Drained canned peas

In large bowl, stir together first 6 ingredients until well blended. Add remaining ingredients and toss to coat well. If peas are preferred, add last. Cover and chill. Best if refrigerated overnight.

POCATELLO HOT POTATO SALAD

Scrub well 9 potatoes. Drop unpeeled into a large saucepan of boiling water. Cover and boil until slight resistance to knife point. Drain; peel and cut into 1/4-inch slices. Set aside, tightly covered. In medium skillet, fry until crisp 1/2 pound bacon (diced). Drain on paper towels. In bacon fat, saute 1/2 cup diced onion. Drain. Add, stirring constantly 1/4 cup white wine or cider vinegar, 1/4 cup water, 1/2 teaspoon salt, 1/4 teaspoon pepper and 2 tablespoons parsley. Pour hot sauce over potatoes, turning gently with fork to coat evenly. Gently stir in bacon. Serve at once. Serve with vegetable, hot bread, and dessert. Yields 6-8 servings.

HANGOVER PASTA SALAD

Cook according to package directions 1 cup (4-ounce) tiny shell macaroni. Drain and rinse with cold water. In a 1 1/2-quart salad bowl, layer in order given:

2 c. shredded lettuce	1 pkg. (10-oz.) frozen English
Cooked macaroni	peas, thawed
2 hard-cooked eggs, sliced	1/2 c. (2 oz.) shredded Swiss
2 slices (1-oz. each) cooked	cheese
ham, cut into thin strips	

Combine and mix well:

1/2 c. mayonnaise	1 tsp. prepared mustard
1/4 c. sour cream	1 tsp. hot sauce
1 T. chopped green onion	

Spread mixture evenly over top of first mixture, sealing to edge of bowl. Sprinkle with 1 teaspoon paprika and chopped fresh parsley. Cover bowl tightly and chill overnight. Do not toss to serve. Yields 6-8 servings.

PEDRO'S MEXICAN SALAD

2 lg. green peppers, cut into 1-inch chunks	4 slices bacon, fried crisp & crumbled
1 med. onion, cut into chunks	4 hard-cooked eggs, sliced
4 med. tomatoes, peeled & cut into chunks	1/2 tsp. salt
1/2 c. celery, chopped	1 tsp. chili powder
	1/2 c. vinegar

Chop vegetables. Fry bacon until crisp; remove. Chop and add to vegetables. To bacon fat in skillet, add vinegar, salt, and chili powder. Mix well and pour over vegetables. Serve on shredded lettuce.

SOUTH TEXAS TACO SALAD

Toss a salad of:

**1 head lettuce, torn to
  bite-sized pieces
2 tomatoes, cut in wedges**

**1/2 green pepper, sliced
1/2 lb. cubed cheddar cheese**

Fry 1 pound hamburger with 1 package dry onion soup and pour over salad. Top with corn chips. Pass a mild taco sauce (bottled) as a dressing. Serves 4-6.

GIT ALONG GAL SALAD

Layer in a large glass compote or serving dish:

**1 pkg. fresh spinach, chopped
1 lb. bacon, baked in oven,
  drained & crumbled
1 pkg. frozen English peas,
  uncooked**

**1 bunch fresh onions, chopped
  with tops
1 head lettuce, chopped
1 doz. boiled eggs, chopped**

**Frost like a cake with a mixture
  of:**

1 c. mayonnaise

1 c. salad dressing

Sprinkle liberally with Parmesan cheese or grated mild Swiss cheese. Cover with plastic wrap and refrigerate for at least 12 hours. Will keep for about a week. Do not toss to serve.

PORKY'S HAM SALAD

**1 (20-oz.) can pineapple chunks,
  packed in unsweetened juice
2 c. uncooked macaroni
1 (10-oz.) pkg. frozen peas
12 oz. cooked ham, diced (about
  2 c.)
2/3 c. sliced green onions**

**1/4 c. dairy sour cream
1/4 c. vegetable oil
2 tsp. Dijon mustard
1 1/4 tsp. ground allspice
1 tsp. salt
1/4 tsp. ground pepper**

Drain pineapple, reserving 1/2 cup juice; set aside. Cook macaroni and peas separately according to directions on packages, omitting salt; drain. In a large bowl, combine ham, green onions, macaroni, peas, and pineapple chunks. In a small bowl, combine sour cream, oil, mustard, allspice, salt, pepper, and pineapple juice. Pour over ham mixture; toss until combined. Cover and refrigerate until well chilled. Serve on lettuce leaves if desired. Makes 8 cups, 4 servings.

SOUTHWESTERN DINNER SALAD

1 lb. ground beef
1/2 tsp. salt
1 med. onion, chopped
1 (15-oz.) can kidney beans,
  drained
1/2 head lettuce, shredded
2 c. taco-flavor tortilla chips
1 c. sharp cheddar cheese,
  shredded
2 soft avocados, peeled, sliced
2 c. ripe olives, pitted
Salad Salsa

In skillet, saute ground beef, salt, and onion. Add drained beans. Heat through. On large plates, layer in order: lettuce, tortilla chips, beef/bean mixture, cheese and Salad Salsa. Repeat. Garnish with avocado slices, ripe olives, cheese, and whole tortilla chips. Makes 6 servings.

Salad Salsa:

1 (8-oz.) can tomato sauce
1/2 med. onion, chopped fine
1/2 med. tomato, cut into small
  pieces
1/4 tsp. salt
1/2 tsp. chili powder

Combine ingredients in saucepan; simmer for 10 minutes.

OLD WEST WESTERN BAKED BEANS

3 c. pinto beans
1 clove garlic, minced
1 or 1 1/2 tsp. salt
2 sm. onions
1/2 c. brown sugar or sorghum
  molasses
1 tsp. chili powder
3/4 c. canned strained tomato
3 or 4 slices bacon or 1/2 c. diced
  salt pork

Wash the beans and cover them with water. Soak them overnight. Remove the beans from water. Heat to boiling point the water in which the beans were soaked. Add the beans, garlic, and salt; simmer 1 hour. Drain the beans, saving the liquid. Place the beans and whole onions in a pot or casserole. Sprinkle the beans with sugar or molasses and chili powder. Cover them with the tomato and 1 cup of the reserved bean liquid. Arrange bacon or diced salt pork or onion slices on top. Cover. Bake in 300° oven for 5 hours.

Robert E. Kerby
8/K

RANCH-STYLE BEANS

2 lbs. pinto or pink beans
2 onions, chopped or thinly
  sliced
2 cloves garlic, finely diced
1/2 tsp. pepper
1/2 tsp. cumin

1 can (4-oz.) diced green chilies
1 can (16-oz.) tomatoes
1 can (7-oz.) taco sauce or chili
  salsa
1 T. salt
1 1/2 tsp. chili powder, opt.

Wash beans. Soak in 3 quarts cold water overnight or bring to a boil in a large kettle. Turn off heat; cover and let stand 1-2 hours. Add enough water if necessary to cover beans by about 2 inches. Boil gently 1 hour. Add remaining ingredients except salt and chili powder. Continue cooking 1-1 1/2 hours, or until beans are tender. Add salt and chili powder.

INDIAN PINTO BEANS

2 1/2 c. pinto beans
7 c. water

1 c. bacon or ham
1 onion, diced

Simmer beans, meat, water, and onion together for 2 1/2-3 hours. (Do not permit to scorch.) Add salt after cooking. Serve as a vegetable.

BACKYARD BEANS

1/2 lb. ground beef
1 can green lima beans
1 can kidney beans
1 can pork & beans
1 T. dry mustard

1/2 c. catsup
1/2 c. brown sugar
4 T. molasses
2 T. vinegar
Dash of salt

Preheat oven to 350°. Brown ground beef. Drain all 3 cans of beans. In a bean pot or covered dish, add browned ground beef, beans, and the rest of the ingredients. Cover and bake at 350° for 30 minutes.

BARBECUE BUTTER BEANS

Wash and put in a large saucepan with lid and cover with water 1 package dried butter beans (large limas) and 1 ham hock. Cook until beans are a little soft. Add:

1/2 c. catsup
1 tsp. chili powder
1 tsp. Worcestershire sauce

2 T. brown sugar
1/2 c. chopped onion
Salt, if needed

Cover and continue cooking until beans are soft and done. It will take about 3 hours. These will need to just simmer slowly. Add more water when necessary.

PICNIC POTATO SALAD

4 c. cubed boiled potatoes
1/2 c. chopped onion
1/2 c. chopped celery
1/2 c. chopped green pepper
1/2 c. grated carrots
1 cucumber, chopped

1 dill pickle, finely chopped
2 tsp. prepared mustard
1/2 tsp. salt
1 tsp. garlic powder
1/2 c. mayonnaise
Paprika

Combine vegetables, mustard, and seasonings. Toss lightly with mayonnaise. Sprinkle with paprika. Yields 12 servings.

PADDY RYAN SOUR CREAM POTATO SALAD

7 med. potatoes (6 c.), cooked in jacket, peeled & sliced
1/3 c. clear French or Italian dressing
3/4 c. sliced celery
1/3 c. sliced green onions & tops
4 hard-cooked eggs

1 c. mayonnaise
1/2 c. dairy sour cream
1 1/2 tsp. prepared horseradish mustard
Salt & celery seed to taste
1/3 c. diced pared cucumber

While potatoes are warm, pour dressing over and then chill for 2 hours. Add celery and onion. Chop egg whites; add. Sieve yolks. Reserve some for garnish. Combine remaining sieved yolk with mayonnaise, sour cream, and horseradish mustard. Fold into salad. Add salt and celery seed to taste. Chill salad for 2 hours. Add diced cucumber; mix. To trim, sprinkle sieved yolk and sliced onion tops over top. Serves 8.

OGALLALA SIOUX SCALLOPED POTATOES

2 lbs. frozen, shredded hash browns (thawed)
2 c. sour cream
1/2 c. butter
1 sm. can cream of chicken soup

1/2 med. onion, chopped
2 c. grated cheese
1 tsp. salt
1/4 tsp. pepper
2 c. cornflakes

In a 9 x 13-inch pan, mix together sour cream, 1/4 cup butter, soup, onion, cheese, salt, and pepper. Add potatoes and mix. Crush cornflakes. Melt 1/4 cup butter. Add to cornflakes. Sprinkle over potato mixture. Bake at 350º for 45 minutes.

OLD-FASHIONED CREAMED POTATOES

Peel and cut fine:

4 potatoes   **1 onion**

Add:

1 green pepper, seeded & chopped

Cook for 5 minutes in a shallow pan in 2 tablespoons butter. Add 1 cup milk. Cook 15 minutes more. Mince with a knife while cooking. Add more milk as it cooks away. When finished, this should be a rich, creamy mass. Add salt and pepper to taste. Stir in 1/2 cup grated cheese and brown the top under the broiler.

HIGH NOON SWEET POTATOES

Peel and boil until tender 2 large sweet potatoes (or use one can). Drain, mash and add 1/2 cup sugar, 3 tablespoons margarine, 2 teaspoons vanilla, 1 cup coconut, and 1/2 cup chopped pecans. Place in a buttered 1-quart casserole. Bake in a 350⁰ oven for 20 minutes. When done, take from oven and place marshmallows on top. Return to oven and toast to a golden brown. Yields 4 servings.

BULL RIDER'S HOMINY CASSEROLE

Drain 1 large can hominy. Add 1 can mushroom soup (undiluted), and 1 can jalapeno peppers (drained and chopped). Top with 1/2 pound Velveeta cheese (grated). Place in greased 1-quart casserole. Cook in a 325⁰ oven for 20 minutes.

TRAPPER'S FRIED RICE

Cook crisp, crumble, and set aside 2 slices bacon. In bacon grease, fry until yolk is hard 1 egg. Remove egg; chop and set aside. Saute in drippings until tender 1/2 cup chopped green pepper and 1/2 cup chopped onion. Add 1 3/4 cups cooked rice. Add crumbled bacon and chopped egg to the other ingredients. Cover with a lid and warm.

PAT'S PLANTATION CASSEROLE

1 lg. eggplant (about 4 c.)
1 beaten egg
1 can cream of mushroom soup
1/3 c. milk

3/4 c. herb stuffing
2 T. melted butter
Cheese

Peel and dice eggplant and boil in 1 cup water with 1 teaspoon salt for 7-8 minutes. Mix egg, soup, milk, and stuffing together. Drain eggplant well. Combine with stuffing mixture and put into a greased casserole. Put 2 tablespoons melted butter on top. Bake at 350° for 30 minutes. Top with cheese.

BUTCH CASSIDY CASSEROLE

2 (10-oz.) pkgs. frozen broccoli
  spears, chopped, thawed
1/2 c. milk
2 T. butter
1/4-3/4 c. sharp cheese, grated

1 c. Minute Rice (may be
  omitted)
1 can cream of mushroom soup
1 sm. onion (1/2 c. chopped
6 soda crackers, crushed

Cook broccoli as directed on package. Drain. Place broccoli in 1 1/2-quart casserole. Combine the rice, cheese, and onion. Add the soup and milk and stir. Pour this mixture over the broccoli. Melt the butter and add cracker crumbs and spread on top. Bake at 350° for 25-35 minutes, or until brown and bubbly. Serves 8-10.

COW CAMP CORN CASSEROLE

1 (16-oz.) can cream-style corn
1 c. milk
2-oz. jar pimento, chopped
1 1/2 c. cracker crumbs
1 sm. pod jalapeno pepper,
  chopped

2 eggs
1/2 stick oleo
1/2 c. longhorn cheese, grated
1/2 c. onion, chopped
Paprika

Mix all of the ingredients except 1/2 cup cracker crumbs and paprika. Pour into a greased 1 1/2-quart casserole or baking dish. Spread remaining cracker crumbs on top and sprinkle with paprika. Bake in oven at 350° for 45 minutes. Serves 6-8.

COUNTRY CABBAGE

Saute until tender 2 chopped onions in 3 tablespoons butter. Add 1 cabbage (cut into wedges) and 2 tomatoes (chopped). Sprinkle with salt and pepper. Cover and cook over low heat for 20-30 minutes, or until cabbage is tender.

SPANISH SQUASH

Dice 3 or 4 yellow squash, 1 medium onion, and 1 can tomatoes (or 2 fresh). Stew with 2 tablespoons margarine until thick. Season with garlic salt, sugar, pepper, and salt. Layer in greased casserole with grated cheese on top. Bake in 350° oven for approximately 15 minutes, or until cheese melts.

ZEKE'S ZUCCHINI CASSEROLE

Saute 1 medium sliced onion in $1/4$ cup salad oil. Add $11/2$-2 pounds sliced zucchini, 3-4 chopped ripe tomatoes, and 1 chopped green pepper. Sprinkle with $1/4$ teaspoon garlic powder and salt and pepper to taste. Cook until tender. Sprinkle with Parmesan cheese and serve.

FRITTER BATTER

Mix and stir until smooth:

1 c. flour	1 T. oil
3 tsp. baking powder	2 eggs, beaten
$1/2$ tsp. salt	$1/3$ c. milk
$1/4$ tsp. sugar	

More liquid may be added if needed. Wash any kind of vegetable. Slice or cut up the way you prefer. Dry **very well** on paper towels. Dip in batter. Fry in hot fat. Drain well. Vegetables that are excellent are:

Squash	Cauliflower
Zucchini	Fresh green onions (leave
Mushrooms	whole)
Onions	Eggplant

Also try cubed cheese. (Have very cold).

Robert E. Kirby
B/K

ROUND-UP WAGON STEW

3¹/₂ lbs. chuck (rump or arm),
  cut in cubes
2 T. flour
2 T. fat
1¹/₂ c. water or consomme

2 med. potatoes, cubed &
  parboiled
3 carrots, sliced
6 sm. onions, peeled

After preparing meat with tenderizer, dust beef cubes with flour. Heat fat in Dutch oven and brown meat in fat. Add water or consomme. Simmer over low heat for about 2 hours. Add vegetables during last 15 minutes and cook until tender.

SLIM PICKENS STEW
(A "Favorite" Among Cowboys Paying Alimony)

2 potatoes
2 carrots
¹/₄ head cabbage
3 sticks celery

1 sm. can tomatoes
2 beef bouillon cubes
1 lb. ground beef
Salt & pepper to taste

Cut vegetables into small pieces and break up ground beef. Put bouillon cubes in two inches of water. Simmer together with vegetables and beef for one hour in 2-pound coffee can. (Serves 3).

INDIAN STEW

2 T. fat
1 onion, chopped
¹/₂ green pepper, chopped
1 lb. lean beef, ground coarse
Pinch chili powder

3 c. fresh corn
1 can tomato soup
2 tsp. sugar
1 tsp. salt

Heat fat in iron skillet and cook onion and pepper until soft. Brown meat. Add remaining ingredients and simmer for 1 hour.

CHUCK WAGON CHOW

1 lb. boneless round or chuck
¹/₂ tsp. salt
2 T. chili powder
¹/₄ tsp. pepper
¹/₃ tsp. garlic powder
2 T. cooking oil

2 sm. onions, chopped
1 green bell pepper, chopped
1 can (15¹/₂-oz.) kidney beans,
  with liquid
1 can (17-oz.) whole-kernel corn,
  with liquid

Cut meat into ³/₄-inch cubes. Season meat with salt, chili powder, pepper, and garlic powder. Brown slowly in cooking oil in medium skillet. Drain off oil. Add onion, green pepper, and liquid from beans and corn. Simmer 45 minutes. Add beans and corn and simmer an additional 15 minutes.

SON OF A BITCH STEW

2 lbs. beef, cut in cubes
6 potatoes
6 carrots
1 cabbage
1 onion
Salt & pepper to taste

Brown meat in Dutch oven in bacon fat. Cover with water and simmer for 1 hour. After an hour, add carrots, salt, and pepper. 30 minutes later, add onion and potatoes. 30 minutes later, add cabbage and cook 15 minutes more. The broth may be thickened when done, if desired, by making a smooth paste of flour and water and adding to stew.

PECOS BILL FIVE-HOUR STEW

2 lbs. meat (chunked steak, round steak, or stew beef)
6 carrots, sliced
4 potatoes, sliced
1 c. celery, cut-up
2 sm. onions, sliced
1 slice bread
2 T. tapioca
1 can whole tomatoes
Salt & pepper to taste

Mix together; put in tightly-covered baking dish and bake in 250° oven for 5 hours.

SOUTHWEST CHILI

1 1/2 lbs. ground beef
1 chopped onion
1 chopped green pepper
1 clove minced garlic
3 (15 1/2-oz.) cans red beans
2 (6-oz.) cans tomato paste
1 T. chili powder
2 tsp. salt

Brown the beef, onion, green pepper, and garlic in a large frying pan. Drain fat. Mix in rest of ingredients. Simmer, uncovered, for 30 minutes. Serves 5.

RIM FIRE CHILI CON CARNE

4 strips bacon
3 onions
2 lbs. ground beef
1 can (1-lb.) tomatoes
1 can (1-lb.) kidney beans
3 T. chili powder
2 tsp. sugar
1/3 tsp. salt
1/4 tsp. pepper
Pinch cayenne pepper
3 garlic cloves

Dice bacon and fry until crisp. Remove bacon and fry onions in fat. Add ground beef and brown. Add tomatoes, beans, chili powder, sugar, salt, pepper, and cayenne. Peel garlic cloves and add. Simmer 15 minutes and remove garlic. Add bacon. Serves 6.

COW CAMP SPECIAL

1/2 c. chopped suet
4 lg. onions, chopped
4 lbs. ground beef
Dash salt & pepper
2 T. chili powder

1 lb. dry kidney beans, cooked tender
2 (#2 1/2) cans (7 c.) tomatoes
2 lbs. noodles, cooked

Heat suet in a skillet and brown onions and beef in it. Season with salt and pepper. Transfer mixture to a large pan. Stir in chili powder, cooked beans, and tomatoes. Cook over low heat for about 40 minutes. Add cooked noodles and simmer until heated.

BUCKHORN SWEET AND SOUR MEATBALLS

2 lbs. hamburger
2 eggs

3/4 c. bread crumbs
Salt & pepper

Sauce:

1 sm. bottle catsup
1 1/2 bottles water (use catsup bottles)

1 onion
2 T. lemon juice
3-4 T. brown sugar

Brown onions in 1/2 tablespoon margarine. Add catsup and water. Boil and add meatballs. Bake at 350° for 1 hour. Remove and add lemon juice and sugar. Place in oven for another hour.

WRANGLER'S SWEDISH MEATBALLS

1 lb. pork & 1 lb. ground beef or 3 lbs. ground beef total
1 c. bread crumbs
1 grated onion
1 c. grated raw potato
2 eggs

1 tsp. brown sugar
1/2 tsp. ginger
1/2 tsp. cloves, ground
2 tsp. salt
1/2 tsp. cinnamon
1/2 tsp. allspice

Mix with hands very well and shape into balls. Roll in flour and place in large pan. Pour milk over them until about half covered. Bake for 1/2 hour and then turn meatballs over and bake for another 1/2 hour. Will serve 18 people. These meatballs do not shrink. Temperature - 350°.

BUNKHOUSE MEAT LOAF

3 lbs. ground beef
1 lb. ground pork
1/2 c. finely-chopped onion
1/2 c. chopped green pepper
1 c. celery, diced
3 eggs

1 c. cooked oatmeal
1 1/2 c. cracker crumbs
1/2 c. ketchup
3 tsp. salt
1/3 tsp. pepper

Mix ingredients. Place in greased loaf pans. Bake at 350° for 1 1/2 hours. Serves 12.

TALL PINES POTATO MEAT LOAF

3 eggs, beaten
2 lbs. ground beef, lean
2 1/2 tsp. salt
1/4 tsp. pepper

2 c. ground raw, pared potatoes,
  firmly packed
1/4-1/2 med.-sized onion, ground
4 slices bacon, ground

Combine ingredients in order listed, mixing thoroughly. Pack into greased 9 1/4 x 5 1/4 x 2 3/4-inch loaf pan. Bake in slow oven (325°) for 1 1/2 hours or until done. Serves 8.

BANDIT'S STUFFED PEPPERS

8 med. green peppers
1 lb. ground beef
1/2 c. chopped onion
1 1/2 c. fresh corn or 1 (12-oz.)
  can whole-kernel corn,
  drained
1 (8-oz.) can seasoned tomato
  sauce

1 tsp. Worcestershire sauce
3/4 tsp. salt
2 c. shredded sharp processed
  cheese
1 c. soft buttered bread crumbs

Cut off tops of green peppers; remove seeds and membranes. Pre-cook pepper cups in boiling salted water about 5 minutes; drain. Sprinkle inside with salt. Brown meat and onion; add next 4 ingredients. Simmer until hot through, about 5 minutes. Add cheese and stir until melted. Stuff peppers; stand upright in 11 x 7 x 1 1/2-inch baking dish. Sprinkle tops with crumbs. Fill baking dish 1/2 inch with water. Bake, uncovered, at 350° for 40 minutes or until hot through. Makes 8 servings.

COUNTRY PEPPERS

6 med. green peppers
1 lb. hamburger, browned
1/4 c. chopped onion

1 1/2 c. cooked rice
1 (8-oz.) jar Cheez Whiz
1/2 c. chopped tomato, opt.

Remove top and seeds from peppers. Parboil 5 minutes; drain. Stir meat, onion, cheese, rice, and tomatoes together. Fill peppers. Place in baking dish; cover. Bake at 350⁰ for 40 minutes. Makes 6 servings. (This is also a good recipe for venison burger.)

SOUTHFORK SUPER SUPPER

1 lb. ground beef
1 med. onion, chopped
1 box beef-flavored stuffing mix
1 can cream of celery soup

1 can cream of mushroom soup
1 soup can water
1 (4-oz.) can mushroom stems & pieces

Brown the beef and onion and drain off fat. Spoon into a 9 x 13-inch baking dish. Scatter the bread cubes over beef mixture. Combine the soups, water, mushrooms, and packet of seasoning mix from stuffing mix in small pan and heat. Pour over ingredients and bake 30 minutes, uncovered, at 350⁰.

RANCH HAND CASSEROLE

Combine the following ingredients without cooking. Place in layers in casserole.

1 lb. ground beef
8-oz. pkg. egg noodles

1 c. chopped celery
1/2 c. chopped onions

Mix and pour the following over the layers:

1 can each (10 1/2-oz.) cream of mushroom and cream of chicken soup

1 1/2 cans water

Bake at 350⁰ for 1 hour and 30 minutes. For variety, add 1 small can French-style green beans, peas, or tomatoes.

HIGH NOON CASSEROLE

1 lb. hamburger
1/2 c. celery, chopped
4 oz. noodles, cooked

1/2 onion, chopped
1/4 c. green pepper, chopped
1 can tomato soup

Brown meat, onion, green pepper, and celery. Cook noodles; drain. Put in casserole with tomato soup. Bake, covered, 1 hour at 350⁰. Yields 4-6 servings.

TOP HAND HASH

2 T. butter
1/4 c. onion, chopped
1/4 c. green pepper, chopped
1 lb. ground beef
1 tsp. salt
1 tsp. chili powder

1/4 c. molasses
1/4 c. prepared mustard
2 T. Worcestershire sauce
1 can (1-lb.) tomatoes
1 c. uncooked rice

Melt butter in skillet. Add onion and green pepper. Cook until onion is tender, but don't brown. Add beef, half of the salt, and chili powder. Brown beef, stirring with a fork. While beef is browning, combine molasses and mustard. Stir in Worcestershire sauce. Add rice slowly. Cover and reduce heat. Simmer until rice is tender.

HAYING CREW'S HAMBURGER SCRAMBLE

1 lb. ground beef
2 T. lard
4 eggs

1 1/2 tsp. salt
1/4 tsp. pepper
1/4 c. chopped onion

Brown meat in lard. Pour off drippings. Beat eggs. Add salt, pepper, and onion. Add egg mixture to meat. Cook slowly, stirring occasionally, until eggs are firm. Serves 4-6.

BOOT HILL BEEF JAMBALAYA

1 lb. lean ground beef
3 T. cooking oil
2 lg. green bell peppers, chopped
1 c. chopped onion
1 clove garlic, mashed
1 can (16-oz.) stewed tomatoes
1 can (8-oz.) tomato sauce

1/4 tsp. paprika
1/2 tsp. chili powder
1/2 tsp. Worcestershire sauce
Few drops Tabasco sauce
Salt & pepper to taste
1 pkg. (1-lb.) frozen shrimp, cooked
1 c. cooked rice

Place cooking oil in Dutch oven or heavy skillet and saute green peppers, onion, and garlic until soft, but not browned. Add ground beef and cook until brown. Drain off excess fat. Add remaining ingredients, except shrimp and rice. Cover and simmer gently, about 20 minutes. Add shrimp and rice and simmer until thoroughly heated. **Variation:** This mixture can also be used for stuffing green peppers. To make stuffed peppers, cut off tops of peppers and discard stem. Remove seeds and white membrane. Parboil peppers; drain and fill with Jambalaya. Top with bread crumbs; place upright in an oiled casserole. Pour 1 cup tomato juice into casserole and bake 20-30 minutes, until peppers are tender. If necessary, just before serving, place under broiler briefly to brown crumbs. This should fill between 8-10 peppers.

GOLD RUSH MEAT AND POTATO PIE

3/4 lb. lean ground beef
1 c. soft bread crumbs
1 egg, beaten
1/2 c. milk
2 T. minced onion
1 tsp. salt

1/8 tsp. pepper
1 tsp. prepared horseradish
2 tsp. catsup
2 c. mashed potatoes
1/2 c. shredded cheddar cheese

Preheat oven to 350°. Combine meat, crumbs, egg, milk, onion, and seasonings. Spread meat mixture in 8-inch pie plate and bake 30 minutes. Drain off fat. Prepare mashed potatoes and spread over meat. Sprinkle with cheese and return to oven until cheese melts.

LONG BRANCH ONE POT DINNER

1 lb. ground beef
3/4 lb. bacon, cut in small pieces
1 c. chopped onion
2 cans (1 lb. 15-oz.) pork &
   beans
1 can (1-lb.) kidney beans,
   drained

1 c. catsup
1 T. liquid smoke
3 T. white vinegar
1 tsp. salt
Dash pepper

Brown ground beef and drain. Cook bacon and onions and drain. Mix all ingredients in a slow cooker and cook for 5-6 hours.

WINNEMUCCA BEEF 'N' POTATO CASSEROLE

4 c. frozen potato rounds
1 lb. ground beef
1 (10-oz.) pkg. chopped broccoli
1 can condensed cream of
   celery soup
1 can (2.8-oz.) French-fried
   onions

1/3 c. milk
1 c. shredded cheddar cheese
1/4 tsp. garlic powder
1/8 tsp. pepper

Place potatoes on bottom and sides of 8 x 12-inch casserole. Bake, uncovered, at 375° for 10 minutes. Brown beef in large chunks. Drain. Place beef, broccoli, 1/2 can onions in potato shell. Combine soup, milk, 1/2 cup cheese, and seasonings. Pour over beef mixture. Bake, covered, at 375° for 20 minutes. Top with remaining onions and cheese. Bake, uncovered, 2-3 minutes.

FIDDLER'S DELIGHT

1 lb. ground beef
1 med. onion, chopped
1½ c. chopped celery
1 (10¾-oz.) cream of tomato
  soup
1 T. catsup

1 tsp. dry mustard
1 tsp. chili powder
1 tsp. Italian seasoning
1 tsp. salt
½ tsp. pepper
1 tsp. Worcestershire sauce

Saute ground beef and onion until lightly browned. Add celery, tomato soup, catsup, and seasonings. Mix thoroughly. Cover and simmer over low heat for 30 minutes. Serve on rice or toasted buns.

LONE PRAIRIE SHEPHERD'S PIE

2 T. oil
1 med. onion, chopped
⅓ c. celery, chopped
1½ lbs. ground beef
1 can beefy mushroom soup

1 pkg. frozen mixed vegetables
Salt & pepper to taste
2 c. seasoned mashed potatoes
1 egg

Brown ground beef; drain off fat. Add all other ingredients except mashed potatoes and egg. Bring to a boil. Pour into greased 1½-quart casserole. Mix egg with seasoned mashed potatoes and spoon over top of casserole. Bake in 325° oven for 30 minutes or until potatoes are lightly browned and mixture is bubbling.

Robert E. Kenby
B/K

CHUCKWAGON CASSEROLE

1 lb. ground beef
1/2 c. chopped celery
1/2 c. chopped onion
1/4 c. chopped green pepper
1 (6-oz.) can tomato paste
1/2 c. water
1 T. chili powder
1 tsp. salt
1 tsp. paprika
1 (17-oz.) can (2 c.) lima beans, drained

1 (16-oz.) can (1 3/4 c.) pork & beans
10 1/2-inch cubes (1 1/2 oz.) American or cheddar cheese
1 (8-oz.) can refrigerated biscuits
2 T. milk
1 c. corn chips, crushed

In 10-inch ovenproof frying pan, brown ground beef, celery, onion, and green pepper; drain. Stir in tomato paste, water, chili powder, salt, paprika, and beans. Simmer while preparing biscuits. Separate biscuit dough into 10 biscuits. Place a cheese cube in center of each biscuit. Fold dough over cheese, covering completely; seal well. Dip biscuits in milk and coat with crushed corn chips. Arrange biscuits around edge of hot meat mixture. Bake 15-20 minutes at 425° until golden brown. Serve immediately. Yields 6-7 servings. **Note:** Hot meat mixture may be transferred to a 12 x 8-inch baking dish or 2-quart casserole. Top with biscuits; bake as directed.

SILVER SPUR STROGANOFF

1 lb. ground beef
1/4 c. chopped onion
1 3/4 c. water
1 can (2-oz.) sliced mushrooms, drained

1 pouch rice & beef flavor sauce
1/2 pt. (8 oz.) sour cream

In large skillet brown ground beef with onion. Add water and bring to a boil; stir in mushrooms and rice and beef sauce. Simmer, uncovered, stirring occasionally, 10 minutes or until rice is tender. Stir in sour cream; heat through, but do not boil. Yields about 4 servings.

JED BARKLEY'S BROCCOLI

Cook according to directions 1 package chopped frozen broccoli. Brown separately 1 pound ground beef and 1 small chopped onion. Add salt and pepper to taste. Spread broccoli in 6 x 9-inch greased baking dish. Top with meat and onion mixture. Cover with 1 can cream of mushroom soup (undiluted). Grate and sprinkle on top 1/2 pound American cheese. Bake in 350° oven until hot through and through. (Or microwave until hot). Yields 6 servings.

SONORA CASSEROLE

Brown 2 pounds ground beef and 1 chopped onion in medium skillet. Add 1 can mushroom soup, 1 can chicken soup, 1 can green chilies (chopped), and 1 small can evaporated milk. Grate 1 pound American cheese. Tear 1 package tortillas (10-12) into pieces. Starting with meat mixture, layer twice in a 2-quart casserole (tortillas, meat, cheese, etc.) End with the cheese. This dish may be made ahead of time and either frozen or refrigerated. Bake in preheated 350⁰ oven for 30 minutes or until bubbly.

RANCHO BEANS

1 lb. pinto or kidney beans
Water to cover
6-8 pork chops
1/4 lb. diced salt pork
1 chopped onion

1 clove minced garlic
1 T. chili powder
1 1/2 tsp. salt
1/4 tsp. pepper

Soak beans overnight in water to cover generously. Cover pot and bring beans to a boil. Reduce heat and simmer until beans are almost tender (about 2 hours). Brown pork chops in fry pan. Remove and set aside. Add salt pork to pan and fry until lightly browned. Add onion and garlic and cook until tender, but not browned. Remove from heat and stir in chili powder, salt, and pepper. Add to beans, mixing well. Arrange browned pork chops on top of beans; cover and simmer 45 minutes longer (or until beans and chops are done). If needed, add a little more water while cooking. (Beans should have a little liquid but should not be soupy). Serves 6.

BUNKHOUSE BEAN BAKE

Use ovenproof skillet to brown 1 pound ground meat and 1/2 pound bacon (chopped). Drain off grease. Stir in:

1 can (14-oz.) baked beans
1 can (14-oz.) kidney beans
1 can (14-oz.) butter beans
1 can (14-oz.) pork and beans
1/2 c. catsup

1 onion, chopped
1 tsp. mustard
1 c. brown sugar
4 T. vinegar

Bake in 350⁰ oven, covered, for 1 hour. Serve with salad and hot bread. Yields 12-14 servings.

LONE RANGER'S BEANS AND RICE

Sort, wash, and soak overnight in water 1 pound pinto beans. The following day, drain and rinse beans and combine with:

2 onions, chopped	1 green pepper, chopped
2 stalks celery, chopped	1 clove garlic, mashed

Put in heavy saucepan and cover with water. Bring to a boil. Reduce heat. Cover and simmer for 1 hour. Add 1 pound smoked sausage, cut into pieces. Continue cooking for 1 1/2 hours, or until beans are tender and a thick gravy is formed. If necessary, add water to prevent beans from sticking. Stir in salt, pepper, Tabasco, and parsley as mixture simmers. Add 2 cups cooked rice last 30 minutes.

LINE CAMP DUMPLINGS

1/4 c. flour	1 egg, beaten
1 tsp. baking powder	1/2 c. milk
1/2 tsp. salt	1 T. butter, melted
1 c. cornmeal	

Add baking powder and salt to flour and sift; mix in cornmeal. Combine egg and milk and add. Mix in melted butter. Drop by spoonfuls into stew. Cover dish and cook for 15 minutes. Serves 6.

RATTLESNAKE GULCH GOULASH

In a large skillet brown together 1 1/2 pounds ground beef and 1 large chopped onion. Season with garlic salt and pepper and 1 teaspoon chili powder (optional). Add 1 can tomatoes. Cook separately in salted water until tender 1/2 bag macaroni. Drain. Add to meat. Simmer for 15 minutes.

CALICO KATE'S HAM-BROCCOLI CASSEROLE

12 slices white bread	6 eggs
10-oz. pkg. frozen broccoli	3 1/2 c. milk
2 c. diced ham	1/4 tsp. dry mustard
3/4 lb. sharp cheddar cheese	Salt & pepper to taste
2 T. minced onion	

Cut circles from center of bread slices and save. Tear bread scraps and put in a buttered 9 x 13-inch casserole. Add broccoli (drained and cooked), diced ham, cheese (shredded), and onion. Place bread circles on top. Add slightly-beaten eggs, milk, salt, pepper, and 1/4 teaspoon dry mustard. Cover and refrigerate overnight. Bake at 325° for 55 minutes, uncovered.

MA'S MACARONI AND CHEESE

Cook in salted water that has come to a rolling boil 1 bag macaroni. Boil until the macaroni is tender. Drain. Cut in chunks and add:

1 lb. Old English or Velveeta cheese	1/2 tsp. salt
1 T. butter	1/4 tsp. pepper

Melt cheese and stir; add a little milk or water if it is too dry.

SOUTH OF THE BORDER TACOS

2 lbs. lean ground beef	Cooking oil
1 tsp. salt	1 head lettuce, shredded
1/2 tsp. pepper	3 lg. onions, diced
1 tsp. garlic powder	3 tomatoes, diced
3 T. chili powder	1/2 lb. longhorn cheese, grated
1/8 tsp. cayenne	Taco sauce or hot sauce
3 doz. corn tortillas	

Blend meat with salt, pepper, garlic powder, chili powder, and cayenne. Brown in heavy skillet, stirring frequently. Drain off fat. In separate skillet, heat tortillas in cooking oil. Drain on absorbent paper. Fill each tortilla with meat, lettuce, onion, and tomato. Top with cheese. Fold and serve with taco sauce.

RUSTLER'S PICK POCKET TACOS

Brown in a skillet:

1 lb. ground beef	1 onion, chopped

Add:

1/2 tsp. salt	1/4 c. chili sauce (more if desired)
1/2 tsp. garlic salt	
2 tsp. chili powder	1/2 tsp. cumin

Cook and stir until all is blended well. Warm pocket bread and fill each with meat mixture, grated cheese, lettuce, and tomatoes. Serve with slices of avocados and picante sauce. Yields 6 servings.

RIM FIRE BEEF BURRITOS

3 lbs. boneless chuck or round
4 T. cooking oil
2 cloves garlic, minced
1 lg. bay leaf, crumbled
Salt to taste
2 med. green bell peppers,
  chopped
1 can (4-oz.) diced green chilies
1 onion, sliced
4 med. tomatoes, cut into 6
  wedges each
Pepper to taste
16 flour tortillas, opt.

Cut meat into ½-inch cubes. Heat oil in large skillet. Add meat, garlic, bay leaf, and salt. Saute until meat is browned. Add green peppers and chilies. Cover and simmer 10 minutes. Add onion and cook 5 minutes. Add tomatoes and pepper and cook 5 minutes. Add a little water if necessary. Spoon into flour tortillas and wrap as burritos by placing about 4 tablespoons meat mixture in tortilla and rolling up. Fasten ends with toothpicks. Tortillas may be homemade or ready-made from store. **Variation:** Instead of filling tortillas, serve with refried beans or rice.

TEX'S TACO BURGERS

Combine:

1 pkg. taco seasoning
¼ c. milk
¼ c. catsup
1½ lbs. ground beef

Mix all together and shape into 6 patties. Grill over hot coals. Serve on hamburger buns with lettuce, tomatoes, onion, and taco sauce. Yields 6 servings.

PANCHO VILLA'S BEEF HASH

1 c. cooked roast beef, chopped
4 cooked potatoes, diced
2 sm. onions, minced
½ c. green peppers, chopped
  (opt.)
1 c. canned tomatoes
1 egg
1 can tomato sauce
Garlic & chili powder to taste
Salt & pepper as desired

Mix all ingredients. Put in baking dish or Dutch oven. Bake about 25 minutes.

LAZY L LASAGNA

1 lb. ground beef
1/4 c. chopped onion
1 (16-oz.) can stewed tomatoes, undrained
1 (6-oz.) can tomato paste
1 tsp. salt
1 tsp. Italian seasoning
1/2 tsp. pepper

1 (4-oz.) can mushroom stems & pieces, drained
10 lasagna noodles
1 (6-oz.) pkg. sliced mozzarella cheese
1 (12-oz.) carton small curd cottage cheese

In heavy 10-inch skillet brown ground beef and onion; drain well. Stir in tomatoes, tomato paste, seasonings, and mushrooms. Heat to boiling. Reduce heat to low; cook, uncovered, for 20 minutes. Meanwhile, cook lasagna noodles according to package directions; drain well. In 11 3/4 x 7 1/2 x 1 3/4-inch baking dish, alternate layers of noodles, mozzarella cheese, cottage cheese, meat sauce, and Parmesan cheese. Bake near center of 350° oven for 25-35 minutes or until hot and bubbly. Allow 5 minutes standing time before serving. Cut into rectangles. **Tip:** Lasagna may be prepared ahead and refrigerated until baking time. Increase baking time 10-12 minutes.

SADDLE UP SPAGHETTI AND MEATBALLS
(Have In Deep Freeze Ready For Guests)

Balls:

Combine and mix well:

1 lb. ground beef
1 egg
1 tsp. salt

1/4 tsp. pepper
1/2 c. crushed crackers

Form into 1 1/2-inch balls and sprinkle with garlic salt. Brown in hot oil. Make spaghetti sauce and meatballs; simmer a few minutes. Serve over cooked spaghetti. Grate cheese and sprinkle on top. Yields 8 servings.

Sauce: Saute 1 cup chopped onion and 1 clove garlic (crushed) in 1/4 cup oil. Add:

1 can (2 lbs. 3-oz.) Italian tomatoes
2 cans (6-oz. each) tomato paste
1/4 tsp. dried oregano leaves
1 tsp. salt

1/8 tsp. pepper
1 tsp. dried basil leaves
2 T. sugar
2 T. chopped parsley
1/2 c. water

Bring to a boil; reduce heat and simmer, covered, 1 1/2 hours. Stir occasionally. Add meatballs and simmer a few minutes. Serve over cooked spaghetti. Top with grated cheese.

HUEVOS RANCHEROS (Mexican Eggs)

1 c. green chili salsa
4 oz. longhorn cheese
4 corn tortillas

4 eggs
Oil & butter for frying

Dip tortillas in heated oil and remove quickly. Set tortillas on baking pan to keep warm. In a frying pan, pan fry eggs in butter until the whites are set, but the yolks are still soft. Put a fried egg on each tortilla. Heat salsa and spoon over each egg. Sprinkle grated cheese on top. Slip baking pan under broiler until cheese melts. **Variation:** Try adding heated refried beans on the tortillas, before topping with eggs, salsa, and cheese.

CORNED BEEF HASH WITH EGGS

1 can (15^1/$_2$-oz.) corned beef
  hash
1 T. minced onion
1 T. minced green bell pepper
2 T. butter or margarine

Dash of Tabasco sauce
Dash of Worcestershire sauce
Salt & pepper to taste
6 eggs

Saute onion and green pepper in butter in a large skillet until onion is soft but not browned. Add hash and mix well. Season with Tabasco, Worcestershire, salt, and pepper. Cook, stirring constantly, until heated through. Smooth out surface and make 6 depressions on top of hash. Break one egg into each depression. Season eggs with salt and pepper. Cover skillet and cook over low heat until eggs are set. Garnish with paprika and serve on toast. **Note:** Substitute diced leftover corned beef and diced cooked potatoes for canned hash.

HASH BROWN SKILLET BREAKFAST

Cook 6 slices bacon in large skillet until crisp. Drain on paper towel. Crumble. Cook in bacon drippings until crisp and lightly browned 1 package frozen hash brown potatoes. Combine and pour over potatoes:

6 eggs, slightly beaten
^{1}/$_2$ c. milk

^{1}/$_2$ tsp. salt
^{1}/$_2$ tsp. pepper

Top with 1 cup grated cheddar cheese. Sprinkle with crumbled bacon bits. Cover and cook over low heat 10 minutes. Cut into wedges and serve warm. Yields 6 servings. **Variation:** Use frozen potatoes with onion, red pepper, and green pepper. Different taste and more colorful.

EGG AND SAUSAGE SOUFFLE

6 eggs, slightly beaten	1/2 tsp. dried oregano leaves
2 c. milk	1 lb. bulk pork sausage,
1 tsp. dry mustard	browned & drained
1 c. baking mix	1 c. shredded cheddar cheese

Mix all ingredients together and cover. Put in refrigerator overnight. Heat oven to 350°. Pour into a greased 2-quart casserole; bake until knife inserted in center comes out clean, about 1 hour. Serves 6.

Robert E. Korby
8/K ©

RANCH RIBS

5-6 lbs. chuck short ribs
1/3 c. soy sauce
1/4 c. honey

1/3 c. Burgundy or claret wine
1 med. onion, sliced

Sauce:

1 sm. onion, chopped
3 T. butter or margarine
1 c. catsup
1 c. chili sauce
Freshly-ground pepper to taste
2 T. liquid smoke

2 T. Worcestershire sauce
2 T. brown sugar
2 T. lemon juice
4 T. honey
1 clove garlic, minced
3-4 T. dry red wine

Preheat oven to 300°. Trim outside fat from ribs and arrange in one layer in a large, shallow baking pan. Mix soy sauce, honey, and wine and pour over ribs. Place onion slices on top. Cover pan with foil. Bake 1 hour. Remove from oven. Drain and discard liquid. While ribs are baking, saute onion in butter until soft, but not browned. Combine with all remaining sauce ingredients and simmer 10-15 minutes. Pour 1/2 of the sauce over cooked ribs. Cover and continue baking 45 minutes. Uncover. Add remaining sauce and continue to bake, uncovered, 30 minutes. Makes 6 servings.

WISHBONE'S BARBECUED SHORT RIBS

2 lbs. lean chuck short ribs
Salt, pepper, & paprika to taste
1 T. cooking oil
1 lg. onion, sliced
1/4 c. catsup

2 T. vinegar
1 tsp. Worcestershire sauce
1/8 tsp. chili powder
1/4 tsp. celery seed

Cut ribs into serving pieces. Season with salt, pepper, and paprika. Heat cooking oil in pressure cooker. Brown ribs with onion. Combine remaining ingredients with 1 cup of water and add to ribs. Put lid on pressure cooker. Bring pressure up to 15 pounds and cook 20-25 minutes. Or, cover and bake in 350° oven 1 1/2-2 hours or until done, basting occasionally.

BAR 7 BARBECUE

3 lbs. beef, stew or chuck roast
2 green peppers, chopped
1/2 c. packed brown sugar
2 T. chili powder
2 tsp. Worcestershire sauce

1 1/2 c. chopped onions
1 (6-oz.) can tomato paste
1/4 c. cider vinegar
2 tsp. salt
1 tsp. dry mustard

Combine the ingredients and put into slow cooker in order given. (Use a 3 1/2 to 5-quart cooker.) Cover and cook on high for 8 hours. With wire whisk, stir mixture until meat is shredded. Serve on long hard buns or hamburger buns. Serves 12.

BIG VALLEY VEAL BARBECUE

5 lbs. veal shoulder
1/2 c. ketchup
1/2 c. onion, chopped

2 lemons, sliced
Salt & pepper

Put veal in roasting pan. Cover with ketchup, onion, and lemon and sprinkle with salt and pepper. Roast in moderate oven at 350⁰ for 3-4 hours or about 45 minutes per pound. Serves 6.

SHORTY'S SHORT RIB DINNER

2 lbs. short ribs of beef
1 tsp. salt
1/4 tsp. pepper
2 c. water

4 potatoes
4 onions
4 carrots
Flour

Brown ribs. Season. Add water. Cover and simmer 1 1/2-2 hours or until tender. About 45 minutes before the end of cooking time, add vegetables. Thicken liquid for gravy. Serves 4.

Robert E. Kerby
BIK

VIRGINIA CITY BEEF BRISKET

3-4 lbs. beef brisket
1/2 bottle liquid smoke
Heavily use garlic salt, onion
  salt, seasoning salt, and
  pepper

Line 9 x 13-inch pan with foil. Place meat in pan. Add seasonings and pour liquid smoke over the top. Seal the foil. Bake at 300° for 1 hour and 15 minutes per pound. After cooking, remove 1 cup of liquid (for barbecue sauce). Discard remaining liquid. Shred the meat with two forks. (It pulls apart easily.) Sprinkle meat with juice of one lemon. Add barbecue sauce to meat and return to oven (300°) for 45 more minutes.

Barbecue Sauce:

1 c. catsup
2 T. Worcestershire sauce
2 T. brown sugar
Dash of Tabasco sauce

COUNTRY-STYLE RIBS AND SAUCE

For about 3 pounds spareribs:

1/2 c. cider vinegar
1/3 c. A-1 steak sauce
2 T. molasses
1 c. catsup
1 env. dry onion soup
1 clove garlic, minced
Dash of pepper
Dash of chili powder
1 c. hot water

Arrange meat in shallow pan and put into preheated 450° oven for 30 minutes. Meanwhile, combine remaining ingredients in a quart jar and shake to blend. Remove meat from oven; drain off fat; reset oven at 350°. Pour sauce over ribs. Return to oven and bake in covered pan for 1 hour, basting several times with sauce in pan. Add a little water if sauce becomes too thick. Ribs should be browned and tender. Sauce thickens as it cooks and they're "derned good."

BILLY THE KID LAMB CHOPS

4 loin lamb chops (1 inch thick)
1/4 c. honey
2 tsp. soy sauce
1/4 c. lemon juice
4 onion slices

Combine soy sauce, honey, and lemon juice. Mix well. Add lamb and chill 1 hour, turning occasionally. Remove lamb. Reserve honey mixture. Broil lamb 3-4 inches from source of heat for 6-7 minutes. Turn and top with onion slices and broil 6-7 minutes longer. Brush lamb with honey mixture frequently during cooking.

BUCKHORN HAM

1 thick-cut ready-to-eat ham
  slice
2 tsp. dry mustard

1/3 c. honey
1/3 c. port wine (or more as
  needed)

Rub ham slice with dry mustard, using 1 teaspoon mustard for each side. Place in a shallow baking pan. Combine honey and wine; pour over ham. Bake, uncovered, in a moderate oven (350⁰) for 35-40 minutes.

PLATTE VALLEY PORK CHOPS

3 T. cooking oil
6 pork chops
Salt & pepper
1/3 c. onion, chopped
1 stalk celery, chopped

2 T. flour
1 1/2 c. water
1/8 tsp. savor salt
1 bay leaf
2/3 c. beer

Heat oil in heavy skillet. Brown pork chops. Remove from pan. Generously salt and pepper each chop. Saute onion and celery in remaining fat. Add flour, stirring until browned. Gradually add water, stirring until well blended. Add pork chops, monosodium glutamate, and bay leaf. Simmer 20 minutes. Add beer and simmer 20 minutes. Serve hot.

RANCH BARBECUE SAUCE

2 med. onions, sliced
3/4 c. ketchup
3/4 c. water
3 T. vinegar
2 T. Worcestershire sauce

1 tsp. salt
1 tsp. paprika
1/4 tsp. black pepper
1 tsp. chili powder

Combine ingredients; heat and use to baste meats or fish. Makes 2 cups.

BOOTHILL BARBECUE SAUCE

1 c. catsup
1/4 c. vinegar
1/4 c. cooking oil
1/4 c. water
1 tsp. chili powder

1/2 tsp. red pepper
1 T. dry mustard
1/2 tsp. salt
1/4 c. sugar
2 cloves garlic, minced

Combine all ingredients in saucepan; bring to boil and simmer for 5 minutes. Meat should be generously basted throughout cooking time. Makes about 2½ cups. This sauce adds a very delicious "sweet and sour" taste to shrimp, chicken, and pork.

COWMAN'S BARBECUED HAMBURGERS

3 T. shortening
3 lbs. ground beef
3 lg. onions, chopped
1 clove garlic, minced
1 T. salt
1 1/2 tsp. pepper

2 tsp. chili powder
2 tsp. Worcestershire sauce
1/4 c. flour
1 1/2 c. canned tomatoes
3/4 c. catsup

Melt shortening in heavy skillet. Combine meat, onions, and garlic. Cook in skillet until lightly browned. Drain grease off and add seasonings. Stir in flour and add tomatoes and catsup. Mix well and simmer 20-30 minutes until thickened. Spoon between split buns to make 20 hot sandwiches.

BARBECUED BEEF SANDWICHES

6 lbs. round roast beef
2 sm. bottles catsup
2 c. brown sugar
2 tsp. prepared mustard
1/4 lb. margarine

1/4 c. Worcestershire sauce
1/2 tsp. chili powder
1/4 tsp. garlic salt
1/4 tsp. onion salt
1/2 c. Coke or 7-Up

Mix ingredients together and heat; then pour over thinly-sliced beef. Simmer for 2 hours in a 200° oven in a 9 x 13-inch covered dish. Can also use a crockpot for heating. Then serve on a bun. **Note:** This is great for entertaining as both the sauce and roast can be prepared a day or two ahead and then just heated up. Roast also slices much easier after being refrigerated.

SADDLE UP CHILI BURGERS

Combine:

1 pkg. chili seasoning mix
1/3 c. milk

1 1/2 lbs. ground beef
1 c. grated cheddar cheese

Mix and shape into 6 patties. Grill over hot coals. Serve on hamburger buns with green pepper slices and additional cheese. Yields 6 servings.

HANGING TREE HAMBURGERS

Combine 4 pounds ground round. Add salt and pepper to taste. Grate 1 medium potato fine and add. Mix well and shape into patties about the size of a hamburger bun and about ³/₄ inch thick. Make 3 or 4 patties per pound. Cook slow on outdoor grill, basting with barbecue sauce. The grated potato keeps the meat from shrinking and stays moist. It also keeps the patties from packing hard. These hamburgers may be cooked ahead and frozen, then heated in the oven or microwave before serving.

CABIN CREEK REUBENS

Take 2 slices of rye bread. Spread one side with Thousand Island dressing or mustard. On bread, place a layer of corned beef (thinly sliced). Top with Swiss cheese slices. Add drained sauerkraut. Spread top and bottom of bread with butter. Cook in hot skillet until golden brown on both sides and cheese is melted. Yields 1 serving.

COCA-COLA COWBOY STEAK

Cut 1 pound round steak in serving pieces. Mix and dip steak into ¹/₂ cup flour, ¹/₂ teaspoon salt, and ¹/₄ teaspoon pepper. Brown in ¹/₄ cup shortening. Cover with 1 medium sliced onion. Add 4 tablespoons catsup and 2 cups Coca-Cola. Simmer on low heat until meat is tender. If it gets too dry, add more Coke or a little water, and continue cooking for about 45-50 minutes, or until done. Yields 4 servings.

BLACK BART'S BARNYARD BONANZA

Mix 2 pounds ground meat, ¹/₂ package dry onion soup mix, and 1 egg. Make into thick patties. Brown in skillet. Pour off grease. Combine and pour over meat 1 can mushroom soup, ¹/₂ package dry onion soup mix, and ¹/₂ can water. Cover and simmer until done. Serve with rice. Yields 8 servings.

RANCH GRILL

3 lbs. sirloin steak, 2 inches thick
1/4 c. olive oil
2 T. soy sauce
1 can (12-oz.) beer
1/2 c. chili sauce
1 T. prepared mustard
1/2 tsp. Tabasco sauce
1 med. onion, chopped
2 cloves garlic, minced
1/8 tsp. liquid smoke
Salt & pepper to taste

In a medium saucepan mix together all ingredients except meat, salt, and pepper. Simmer about 30 minutes. Coat meat with sauce on both sides, reserving remainder of sauce. Grill steak over hot coals to desired doneness, basting frequently. Remove to warm platter and season with salt and pepper. Reheat remaining sauce and serve as gravy.

TEAM ROPER'S STEAK FINGERS

1 1/2 lbs. round tip steak
1/2 c. tomato juice
1/2 c. vinegar
1 tsp. salt
1 tsp. pepper
2 c. flour or cornmeal
3 T. cooking oil
1 sm. clove garlic (crushed), opt.

Trim meat to finger lengths, about 1/4 inch thick and 1/2 inch wide. Mix tomato juice, vinegar, salt, pepper, and garlic. Dip meat in mixture, then roll in flour. Saute on both sides in medium skillet in cooking oil, 6-8 pieces at a time, 2 or 3 minutes to desired doneness. Serve with hot barbecue sauce. Makes 4 servings.

CHUCKWAGON CHUCK STEAKS

2 beef blade steaks, cut 1/2-3/4 inch thick
1 med.-sized onion, chopped
1 c. catsup
1/3 c. vinegar
2 T. brown sugar
2 tsp. salt
1 clove garlic, crushed
1 bay leaf
1/8 tsp. hot pepper sauce

Combine onion, catsup, vinegar, brown sugar, salt, garlic, bay leaf, and hot sauce in saucepan and cook slowly 10 minutes, stirring occasionally. Cool. Pour sauce over steaks in a glass dish, turning to coat all sides. Marinate in refrigerator overnight. Pour off and reserve marinade. Place steaks on grill and broil for 20-25 minutes. Turn and brush steaks with sauce occasionally. (This recipe should be doubled to serve 4.)

WILD BILL'S SPECIAL CHUCK STEAK

2 lbs. chuck eye steak, 1¹/₂
  inches thick
1 T. cooking oil
Salt & pepper to taste
1 med. onion, chopped
1 lg. clove garlic, chopped
1 tomato, chopped

1 lg. rib celery
Several celery leaves
1 carrot, sliced
2 green onions, chopped
1 T. lemon juice
2 T. orange juice
1 T. flour

In heavy skillet or Dutch oven, brown meat in oil. Remove meat and season with salt and pepper. In the same skillet, saute onion and garlic until onion is soft, but not browned. Pour off oil. Return the meat to skillet. Add ³/₄ cup of water and remaining ingredients except flour. Let come to a boil. Lower heat and simmer 1¹/₂-2 hours. Remove meat to warm platter and thicken gravy with 1 tablespoon flour mixed with ¹/₄ cup water.

CAMP COOK BEEF STEAK (Mexican Style)

Take boneless steaks about 6 or 8 ounces each. Pound 1 level teaspoon of Mexican chili powder into each steak. Season with salt and roll in cornmeal, pressing the meal into each beaten steak. Put bacon fat into large frying pan or Dutch oven and let get hot. Place steaks in pan and fry until done. Mix 1 cup minced onions, 1 teaspoon minced garlic, 2 cups thick tomato sauce, 2 cups hot water, 1 teaspoon Mexican chili powder, and salt to taste. Pour over steaks and simmer until onions are done. Serve steaks with sauce. Goes fine with rice or tortillas.

BRONC RIDERS GREEN PEPPER STEAK AND RICE

1¹/₂ lbs. boneless round steak
  (cut into strips ¹/₂ inch thick)
1 T. paprika
2 T. butter
¹/₂ c. Burgundy or other red
  wine
2 tsp. each garlic powder and
  salt

¹/₄ tsp. pepper
1 T. cornstarch
¹/₄ c. water
1 c. chopped green onions
2 c. green pepper strips
2 lg. fresh tomatoes, diced
3 c. hot cooked rice

Sprinkle steak with paprika. Brown meat rapidly using high heat, on all sides. Reduce heat. Add wine, soy sauce, and seasoning. Cover and simmer 25 minutes. Blend cornstarch and water. Stir into meat. Arrange onions, green peppers, and tomatoes over steak. Replace cover and simmer 10-15 minutes longer. Serve over beds of fluffy rice. Makes 6 servings.

CHISHOLM TRAIL CORNED BEEF

5-lb. brisket
1½ c. coarse salt
½ oz. saltpeter
1 T. brown sugar
9 bay leaves, crumbled, divided

2 T. pickling spices
8 cloves garlic, divided
1 onion, sliced
½ c. vinegar

Combine 4 quarts of water, salt, saltpeter, brown sugar, 6 bay leaves, and pickling spices. Boil 5 minutes, then cool. Place beef in large glass or stoneware crock. Add boiled mixture and 6 cloves garlic, slivered. Add extra water if needed to cover meat completely. Place heavy plate over meat and add weight to keep meat submerged. Tie a piece of muslin over top of crock. Muslin should be taut and tightly tied. Cover crock, leaving a gap to allow some air circulation. Let crock stand in cool place 2 weeks. At end of 2 weeks, rinse meat well and place in Dutch oven. Add fresh water to 1 inch above meat. Add 3 bay leaves, 2 cloves chopped garlic, onion, and vinegar. Bring to boil. Reduce heat and simmer until meat is tender, 2½-3 hours. Allow meat to stand, covered, 30 minutes. Drain well. Trim off fat and thinly slice meat.

SADDLEPACK JERKY

Slice beef or deer steak as thin as possible, no thicker than ¼ inch. Cut diagonally across the grain of meat. Put in a jar and shake until mixed:

2 tsp. salt
⅔ tsp. MSG
½ tsp. Accent
2 tsp. liquid smoke
½ c. Worcestershire sauce

½ c. soy sauce
2 tsp. onion powder
1 tsp. coarse black pepper (use
more for hotter jerky)
⅔ tsp. garlic powder

Marinate overnight. Place in 200° oven on cookie sheets. Bake 8-10 hours, turning meat several times. Store in plastic bags or covered glass containers. Yields approximately 3 pounds.

BRONCO BILLY'S BEEF JERKY

1½ lbs. beef
¼ c. soy sauce
1 T. Worcestershire sauce
1 tsp. tenderquick
¼ tsp. pepper

¼ tsp. garlic powder
¼ tsp. onion powder
2 tsp. liquid smoke
2 tsp. Tabasco

Cut beef in strips ⅛-¼ inch thick and about 1½ inches wide. Mix all ingredients, sauces, and spices. Pour over beef strips. Keep in a cool place overnight in a covered container. Place marinated beef strips in racks in cookie sheets in 200° oven for 4-5 hours. Cool. Store in covered container.

KIT CARSON BEEF JERKY

Cut beef or venison in foot-long strips. Must be cut with grain for stringiness. Make a strong salt and water solution. Dip meat strips into brine until meat is white. Lay strips in the sun. Meat must hang until thoroughly dry. Store strips in container with holes in cover, or use cloth sacks to allow air to penetrate to meat. Meat can be eaten as jerky or simmered in stew pot.

JERKY GRAVY

4 c. beef jerky pieces	**3 T. flour**
3 T. fat	**2 c. milk**

Pound jerky pieces into flakes and powder. Use a heavy wooden mallet or hammer. Put pounded meat in Dutch oven with the fat. Over low heat, blend flour into fat. Cook and stir until the flour has thickened. Continue to cook slowly and stir constantly while adding the milk. Cook over moderate heat, stirring constantly, until thickened. This gravy will probably not need seasoning as jerky will have retained its salt and pepper. Serve on hot Dutch oven biscuits, or on plain boiled potatoes with jackets. Jerky is good on rice, boiled macaroni, or mashed potatoes.

RANGE RIDER ROAST AND GRAVY

Tear foil large enough to completely wrap a 3 or 4 pound chuck or shoulder roast. Sprinkle with a little salt and pepper. Place roast on foil and spread with 1 can cream of mushroom soup (undiluted). Sprinkle with 1 package dry onion soup mix. Wrap tightly and place in pan. Bake in preheated 300° oven for 2¹/₂-3 hours. Yields 6-8 servings.

ROBBERS' ROOST ROAST

Use either prime rib, rolled or rump roast (any size) and salt and pepper. Place in a roasting pan on a rack, uncovered, in a preheated 375° oven for 1 hour. (Do this in mid-afternoon.) After 1 hour, turn off the oven, but **do not open** the oven door. **For rare roast beef:** 40 minutes before serving time, turn oven to 300°. **For medium roast beef:** 50 minutes before serving time, turn oven to 300°. **For medium-well roast beef:** 55 minutes before serving time, turn oven to 300°.

OLD FAITHFUL POT ROAST

Sprinkle generously 4 pound roast of your choice with seasoned salt. Place in uncovered heavy deep pan. Place in hot oven and sear, turning to brown all sides. When very lightly browned, pour in 2 cups water. Reduce heat to 300º and cover with lid. Cook 1¹/₂-2 hours. Add 3 quartered potatoes, 3 quartered onions, and 3 quartered carrots. Season vegetables with salt and pepper. Continue cooking for 1 hour or longer. Remove roast and vegetables to a platter and make Roast Gravy.

Roast Gravy:

2-3 T. flour

¹/₂ c. water

Salt & pepper

¹/₄ tsp. chili powder

Mix together. Stir into liquid from roast. Cook and stir until slightly thickened. This is one that you will need to taste to get the flavor you want.

WESTERN KANSAS KABOBS

2 lbs. boneless steak

¹/₂ c. soy sauce

¹/₂ tsp. ginger

2 T. salad oil

1 T. sugar

1 c. pineapple chunks, drained, or fresh pineapple

1 basket cherry tomatoes

Cut meat into 1-inch cubes. Pierce meat with fork so marinade can penetrate. Combine soy sauce, ginger, salad oil, and sugar. Pour over meat cubes. Allow to stand for at least 1 hour. Turn occasionally. Put meat on skewers, leaving space between pieces. Put pineapple chunks and tomatoes on other skewers. Broil meat over hot coals. When meat is turned, add skewers of pineapple and tomatoes to the grill. Brush skewers of food with marinade.

ROCKY MOUNTAIN OYSTERS

12 medium-sized mountain oysters

1 egg, beaten

1 c. light cream

3 c. crushed cracker crumbs

4 T. butter or margarine

Wash oysters well and simmer briefly in water to cover. Remove all loose skin or membrane. Split so they will lie flat. Soak in cold water 2-3 hours. Dip in mixture of egg and cream. Roll in cracker crumbs. Saute quickly in butter at high heat until crisp. **Variation:** Mix together in a bag 1 cup flour, 1 teaspoon salt, and ¹/₂ teaspoon pepper. Shake oysters in flour. Mix until thoroughly coated, then saute in butter.

WYATT EARP BOILED TONGUE

Fresh: Wash tongue thoroughly and place in large kettle. Cover with salted water (1 teaspoon salt for each quart of water). If desired, add an onion (cut in quarters), a sprig of parsley, 1 or 2 bay leaves, several peppercorns or cloves, a stalk of celery, or, for variety, 1/4 cup brown sugar, 1 small orange (cut in half), 1 tablespoon whole allspice or pickling spice, 1 hot pepper from pickling spice. Simmer until tongue is tender (3-4 hours or about 1 hour per pound). When tender, plunge into cold water. Remove skin and trim root ends. To serve cold, cool in cooking liquid after skinning. **Smoked:** Soak tongue overnight in cold water. Drain and cover with fresh cold water. Bring to a boil and discard water. Cover with hot water and cook as for fresh tongue. **Quick Method:** Pressure cook 40 minutes at 10 pounds pressure. Reduce pressure gradually.

DIXIE FRIED CHICKEN

1 (2 or 3 lb.) cut-up chicken	2 c. plain flour
Salt	1 tsp. red pepper
Pepper	1 beaten egg
1/2 c. milk	HOT oil

Salt and pepper chicken. Combine flour and red pepper. Set aside. Combine egg and milk. Dip chicken in egg mixture. Then dredge in flour, coating well. Place chicken in oil. Cover and cook over medium heat for 30 minutes or until brown. Drain good on paper towels.

WILL JAMES TAILGATE CHICKEN

1 fryer, cleaned & cut-up	1 1/2 c. crushed potato chips*
1 stick melted butter	1/4 tsp. garlic powder

*You may want to try barbecue or sour cream and onion chips for a totally different flavor. Preheat oven to 325°. Dip chicken in melted butter. Roll in crushed potato chips and garlic powder. Bake on cookie sheet for 50 minutes in 325° oven.

COUNTRY-FRIED CHICKEN

1 c. all-purpose flour	1/4 tsp. poultry seasoning
2 tsp. garlic salt	1/2 c. milk
2 tsp. MSG	1 egg, lightly beaten
1 tsp. black pepper	1 frying chicken, cut-up
1 tsp. paprika	Shortening for frying

Combine flour, garlic salt, MSG, pepper, paprika, and poultry seasoning in plastic bag. Shake chicken. Combine milk and egg. Dip chicken pieces in mixture. Shake chicken a second time in the seasoned flour. Pan fry or deep fry. Drain on paper towels.

LONE PINE CHICKEN WITH CORNMEAL DUMPLINGS

1 stewing hen, cut-up	Salt
Pepper	2 carrots, sliced
2 onions, sliced	2 c. cornmeal
1 tsp. salt	2 eggs.²/₃ c. milk
2 tsp. baking powder	

Put chicken in Dutch oven, including giblets. Add carrots, onions, salt, and pepper. Cover well with boiling water. Simmer for 1½ hours until tender. Mix meal, salt, and baking powder. Beat eggs and milk together and add to meal mixture until dough is stiff. Add more meal if needed. Remove chicken from broth but keep warm. Drop dough by spoonfuls into boiling broth. Cover lightly and simmer for 15 minutes. Serve together.

PRAIRIE SCHOONER SUNDAY DINNER

²/₃ c. uncooked rice (or 1¹/₃ c. Minute Rice), uncooked	¹/₂ c. milk
1 can cream of mushroom soup	1 pkg. dry onion soup
1 can cream of celery soup	1 cut-up fryer or 6 pork chops

Mix above ingredients (except meat and dry soup) and heat to boiling, but do not boil. Pour into greased casserole. Lay pieces of raw meat over rice. Sprinkle dry soup over meat. Bake at 325° for 2½ hours (do not preheat).

RALPH'S HUSH PUPPY MIX

Mix in a large bowl:

8 c. flour	2¹/₂ T. sugar
8 c. cornmeal	2 T. salt
5 T. baking powder	

Keep in an airtight container. Store in refrigerator. To mix, take out amount needed; add milk to make a thick batter. (Add chopped onions, if desired). Drop by teaspoonfuls into hot oil (1-1½ inches deep). When brown, remove and drain on paper towels. Serve warm. **Yield:** Complete recipe will serve about 50 people, 1½ cups of mix, about 4 people.

FLATLANDER'S FISH FILLETS

6 fish fillets
6 slices bacon, partially cooked
6-oz. tiny shrimp, drained
6 tomato slices

2 oz. (1/2 c.) shredded cheddar
 cheese
2 tsp. chopped chives

Butter Sauce:

3 T. butter, melted
1 T. lemon juice
1 1/2 tsp. Worcestershire sauce

1/2 tsp. prepared mustard
1/2 tsp. salt

In small bowl combine all sauce ingredients; set aside. Heat oven to 350°. Arrange fillets in 11 x 17 or 13 x 9-inch pan or baking dish. Place bacon slices on fillets; top with heaping teaspoonful of shrimp. Spoon half of sauce on fillets. Bake at 350° for 20 minutes. Place tomato slices on fillets; sprinkle with cheese. Pour remaining sauce on fillets; continue baking 10-15 minutes or until cheese melts and fish flakes easily with fork. Sprinkle with chopped chives. Yields 6 servings.

LAKE TAHOE TROUT

6 fillets of trout (or any other
 thin white fillets)
1 c. milk
1/2 c. flour

Salt, pepper to taste
1/2 lb. butter
3 T. lemon juice
1/4 lb. sliced almonds

Dip each fillet in the milk, then lightly dust with salt and pepper. Melt the butter in a large, heavy skillet. Brown the fillets on both sides. Remove the fish and keep warm. Add the lemon juice and almonds to the skillet. Quickly bring the mixture to a boil. Stir constantly, scraping the bottom of the pan. When the almonds are golden, pour the mixture over the fillets. Serve immediately. Makes 6 portions.

GRILLED FISH FILLETS

6 (3/4-inch thick) fish fillets
 (flounder, halibut, red
 snapper)
1/2 c. butter or margarine
1/4 c. lemon juice

1 T. Worcestershire sauce
1/2 tsp. seasoned salt
1/2 tsp. paprika
1/4 tsp. red pepper

Place fillets in large shallow pan. Combine remaining ingredients in a small saucepan; cook, stirring constantly, until butter melts. Pour marinade over fish. Cover; marinate 1 hour in refrigerator, turning once. Drain fillets, reserving marinade; place fillets on aluminum foil which has been slitted on the bottom. Grill over hot coals, 3-5 minutes on each side, basting often with marinade. Fish is done if it flakes easily when tested with a fork.

BARBECUED SHRIMP

1 c. oil
1 T. brown sugar
1 T. salt
1 T. dry mustard

1 T. Worcestershire sauce
1/4 tsp. liquid smoke
1/2 c. Burgundy wine

For marinade, combine all ingredients in flat pan and mix thoroughly. Peel and split raw shrimp and marinate for half an hour. Remove shrimp and broil over charcoal fire. Serve with cocktail sauce.

ANDY'S BAKED SALMON

1/3 c. mayonnaise
2 T. lemon juice
1/2 tsp. curry powder
Pepper to taste
2 c. (1-lb. can) red salmon
2 coarsely-chopped hard-boiled
  eggs
Paprika

2/3 c. (small can) undiluted
  evaporated milk
1 T. grated onion
1/4 tsp. salt
1 tsp. parsley flakes
1 c. finely-chopped celery
3/4 c. soft bread crumbs

Mix mayonnaise, evaporated milk, lemon juice, and seasonings. Remove skin and bones from salmon. Break into large pieces. Toss with celery, eggs, and mayonnaise mixture. Pour into buttered 1-quart casserole. Top with crumbs and paprika. Bake at 350° for 35 minutes or until hot and browned.

FIRESIDE FISH AND VEGETABLE STEW

Vegetable cooking spray
1/2 c. chopped celery
1 (16-oz.) can tomatoes,
  undrained & chopped
1 T. Worcestershire
1/2 tsp. pepper & salt
1 c. sliced carrots
1 c. frozen lima beans

1 c. chopped onion
1 lg. clove garlic, minced
2 T. malt vinegar
1/2 tsp. dried whole basil
2/3 c. water
1 c. frozen corn
1 (16 oz.) fish fillets, cut into
  bite-sized pieces

Coat a Dutch oven with cooking spray; place over medium heat until hot. Add onion, celery, and garlic; saute until tender. Stir in tomatoes, vinegar, Worcestershire, basil, salt, pepper, and water. Bring to a boil. Add remaining ingredients. Cover; reduce heat and simmer 20 minutes, stirring occasionally. Good over wild rice.

Robert E. Kerby

BREADS AND ROLLS

JAN'S SOURDOUGH STARTER

2 pkgs. dry yeast (or 2 cakes yeast)	2 c. warm water
	2 c. flour

Dissolve yeast in warm water. Add flour. This will produce a syrupy batter. Cover loosely and place in warm spot overnight. Never add anything else to this excepting 2 cups warm water and 2 cups flour the night before you get ready to use it again. This will insure a continual supply. Always keep half of the starter. Keep it refrigerated until night before you are ready to use. The longer you keep it, the better the starter is. You can retain the initial starter as much as 10 years as did our ancestors.

SOURDOUGH PANCAKES-1

2 c. starter	4 T. cooking oil
1 egg	1 tsp. soda
2 T. sugar	1 tsp. salt

Mix the starter, egg, sugar, and oil well. Add soda and salt last. Serve with warm syrup, honey, or jelly.

SOURDOUGH PANCAKES -2

1/2 c. sourdough starter	2 eggs
1 c. undiluted evaporated milk	2 T. sugar
1 c. warm water	1/2 tsp. salt
1 3/4-2 c. unsifted flour	About 1 tsp. soda

Combine starter, evaporated milk, water, and flour in a large bowl. Mix to blend and leave at room temperature overnight. The next morning, add eggs, sugar, salt, and soda and mix well (don't beat)! Cook on a greased griddle over moderate heat. Do not let griddle smoke! Turn when top side is full of broken bubbles and has lost glossiness. Makes 30 dollar-size or a dozen 6-inch pancakes.

SUNRISE SOURDOUGH BUCKWHEATS

Follow pancake recipe #2, but in place of the flour called for, substitute 1½ cups buckwheat flour and ¼-½ cup white flour.

SADDLE PACK FLAPJACKS

2 c. sifted flour	2 eggs, separated
3 tsp. baking powder	1 1/2 c. milk
3/4 tsp. salt	2 T. melted butter
1 T. sugar	

Sift dry ingredients together; beat egg yolks. Add milk and melted butter and add gradually to dry ingredients, beating well to obtain a smooth mixture. Fold in the stiffly-beaten egg whites. Drop from spoon onto hot greased griddle and brown on both sides.

SALISAW SOUR DOUGH BREAD

1 pkg. active dry yeast in 1 c. warm water	2 T. salt
	1 1/2 c. starter (room temp.)
2 T. sugar	4 c. regular all-purpose flour

Put 1 cup warm water in warm bowl and sprinkle with yeast. Stir in next 3 ingredients. Add flour and mix. Cover bowl and let rise 1 hour and knead 10 minutes. Make into 2 loaves. Let rise 40 minutes. Bake at 400° for 30-35 minutes.

WAGON TRAIN WHEAT BREAD

Dissolve together 2 packages dry yeast and 2 cups lukewarm water. Add 3/4 cup oil and 1/2 cup sugar or honey. Sift together 2 cups flour, 4 cups whole-wheat flour, 1 tablespoon salt, and 1/2 cup dry milk.

Mix well and knead 5 or 6 times. Put in a greased bowl and cover with a cloth. Let rise at room temperature until double in size. Punch down; divide dough into two parts. Put in 2 greased loaf pans and let rise again (about 2 hours). Bake in preheated 400° oven for 25-30 minutes. Yields 2 loaves.

HIAWATHA'S WHOLE-WHEAT BREAD

3 c. warm water	5 1/2 c. stoneground whole-wheat flour
3/4 c. honey	
2 pkgs. yeast	1 scant T. salt
1/4 c. salad oil	2-3 c. white flour

In a large bowl combine water, honey (honey may be reduced to 1/2 cup if desired) and yeast and allow to soften for 5 minutes. Add oil, wheat flour, and salt and beat well. Stir in white flour. Knead and let rise. Knead again and let rise. Knead and make into loaves. Bake at 350° for 50 minutes.

BROKEN BOW BROWN BREAD

1/2 c. flour
1/2 c. whole-wheat flour
1/2 c. yellow cornmeal
1 tsp. soda
1/4 tsp. salt

1/2 c. raisins or chopped dates
1 c. buttermilk
1/3 c. dark molasses
1/4 c. oil

Combine all ingredients and mix well. Pour 1 1/3 cups of batter into 2-cup glass measuring cup and microwave 6-8 minutes on half power. Repeat with remainder of batter. Makes 2 round loaves. Serve while hot.

"MESA" HUSH PUPPIES

Combine:

1/2 c. flour
2 tsp. baking powder
1 T. sugar

1/2 tsp. salt
1 1/2 c. cornmeal
Garlic salt, opt.

Add:

1 egg
3/4 c. milk

1/2 c. finely-chopped onion, opt.

Stir only to moisten. Drop batter by teaspoonfuls into deep hot fat. Fry only a few at a time. Cook until golden brown on both sides. Drain on paper towels. Yields 2 dozen.

PONDEROSA POPPY SEED BREAD

1 box yellow cake mix
1 pkg. instant coconut pudding
  mix
4 eggs

1 c. hot water
1/2 c. liquid shortening
1/4 c. poppy seed

Mix dry ingredients. Add water and liquid shortening. Add eggs, one at a time, beating well after each addition. Pour into 2 loaf pans (greased). Bake at 350° for 40 minutes.

SOURDOUGH CORNBREAD

1 c. sourdough starter
1 1/2 c. yellow cornmeal
1 1/2 c. evaporated milk
2 eggs, beaten

2 T. sugar
1/4 c. melted butter (warm)
1/2 tsp. salt
About 3/4 tsp. soda

Thoroughly mix the starter, cornmeal, evaporated milk, eggs, and sugar in a large bowl. Stir in melted butter, salt, and soda. Turn into 10-inch greased pan and bake in hot oven (450°) for 30 minutes. Serve hot.

MEXICAN CORNBREAD

1 c. cornmeal
1 can (17-oz.) cream-style corn
or whole-kernel corn, drained
3/4 c. milk
1/2 tsp. baking soda
1/3 c. butter or margarine,
melted
1 tsp. salt
2 eggs, slightly beaten
2 c. grated sharp cheddar
cheese
1 can (4-oz.) diced green chilies

Preheat oven to 400°. Combine all ingredients in a large bowl and mix well. Pour batter into a greased 9 x 9-inch baking dish. Bake 30 minutes.

NAVAJO CAKE

6 c. water
4 c. precooked blue cornmeal
2 c. precooked yellow cornmeal
1/2 c. raisins
1 c. sprouted wheat
1/2 c. brown sugar

Put 6 cups water in pan and boil. Add 4 cups precooked blue cornmeal. Add 2 cups precooked yellow cornmeal. Add 1/2 cup raisins. Add 1 cup sprouted wheat. Add 1/2 cup brown sugar. Blend well. Dissolve all lumps. Pour into baking pan that is lined with foil. Cover with foil. Bake at 250° for 4 hours. Cake must bake slowly.

SQUAW BREAD

2 c. flour
1 tsp. salt
2 tsp. baking powder
1/2 c. powdered milk
1 T. sugar
1 c. warm water (approx.)

Combine dry ingredients in a bowl. Gradually add enough warm water to make a soft dough. Divide dough in half and turn out on lightly-floured surface. Pat into 8-inch circles about 1/2 inch thick. Cut into pie-shaped wedges. Slit center of each wedge. Fry quickly in deep hot fat (375°) or in approximately two inches hot fat or oil. Drain on absorbent paper. While warm, dust with powdered sugar. (Dough that is overhandled will tend to make tough bread.)

TRADING POST ORANGE-APRICOT BREAD

1/2 c. dried apricots	1 tsp. vanilla
1 orange	1 egg
1/2 c. raisins	2 c. sifted flour
1/2 c. chopped nuts	2 tsp. baking powder
2 tsp. butter	1/4 tsp. soda
1 1/3 c. sugar	1/4 tsp. salt

Soak apricots in enough cold water to cover for 1/2 hour. Squeeze juice from orange into a measuring cup and add enough boiling water to make a cup. Put orange skins, drained apricots, and raisins through a food chopper. Cream butter and sugar. Add vanilla, egg, and fruit mixture and beat smooth. Add dry ingredients alternately with orange juice and water, blending after each addition. Bake at 350° an hour in a greased and floured pan (9 x 5 inches).

CALICO KATE'S COFFEE CAKE

3 c. sifted flour	1 c. milk
1/2 tsp. salt	1 c. brown sugar
3 tsp. baking powder	2 T. butter
1/2 c. butter	2 T. flour
1 1/2 c. sugar	1 tsp. ground cinnamon
1 tsp. vanilla	1 c. chopped walnuts
4 eggs	

Sift together dry ingredients. Cream together 1/2 cup butter and sugar until light and fluffy. Add vanilla and eggs, beating well. Add dry ingredients alternately with milk, blending well after each addition. Spread 1/2 of batter in greased 13 x 9 x 2-inch pan. Combine remaining ingredients. Sprinkle 1/2 of mixture over batter. Spread with remaining batter; top with remaining crumbs. Bake in 350° oven for 45 minutes or until done. Makes 12 servings.

CABIN FEVER COFFEE CAKE

1 pkg. yellow cake mix	1 1/2 c. (12 oz.) dairy sour cream
1 c. brown sugar (packed)	1/4 c. firm butter
3 eggs	3/4 c. chopped walnuts

Heat oven to 350°. Measure 2/3 cup of cake mix (dry) in small bowl. Cut in butter. Mix in sugar and walnuts. Set aside. Beat eggs lightly with a fork; stir in sour cream. Blend in remaining dry cake mix, scraping bowl often. Batter will be thick and lumpy. Pour half of batter into greased and floured oblong pan (13 x 9 inches). Sprinkle half of topping over batter. Spoon and gently spread remaining batter into pan. Top with remaining topping mix. Bake 40-45 minutes. Cool and spread with thin powdered sugar icing.

63

OLD-TIME BUTTERMILK BISCUITS

Sift dry ingredients together:

2 c. flour	**4 tsp. baking powder**
1/2 tsp. salt	**1/2 tsp. soda**

Cut 5 tablespoons shortening in with pastry blender. Add 1 cup buttermilk all at once. Stir with a fork until dough makes a ball. Turn out on floured board and knead 5 or 6 times. Roll out on lightly-floured board until about 1/2 inch thick. Brush with melted butter. Fold over and cut about 2-inch biscuits. Bake on a very lightly-greased cookie sheet, or spray sheet with spray shortening. If you like your biscuits to be brown all around, don't let them touch each other. If you prefer fatter biscuits, put them close together. Bake in preheated 450° oven for 12-15 minutes.

SOURDOUGH BISCUITS

To prepare this cowboy favorite, you'll need a starter. Soak a half cake of yeast in a half cup of lukewarm water until the yeast is soft. Mix the yeast and water with a half cup of lukewarm water, adding enough flour to make a thick batter. Stir thoroughly. Put mixture into a jar. Cover and place in a warm spot. After 24 hours, mix in another half cup of lukewarm water, a teaspoonful of sugar, and enough flour to make a thick batter. Let batter stand overnight. To make biscuits, use most of the starter, mixing a half teaspoon of soda, a dash of salt, and enough flour to make a thick dough. Knead thoroughly. Pinch off dough in desired size; dip tops in fat and place in Dutch oven or baking pan. Keep some of the starter in the jar; add lukewarm water and enough flour to make a thick batter. Store until needed.

NEVER-FAIL SOURDOUGH BISCUITS

1½ c. flour	**1/2 tsp. salt**
2 tsp. baking powder	**1/4 c. melted butter**
1/4 tsp. baking soda	**1 c. sourdough starter batter (see above or page 59)**

Sift the dry ingredients together. Blend in butter and starter. Pat the dough out on a floured surface, add a little more flour, if necessary. Cut in rounds or squares and place on greased baking sheets. Cover and let rise 30 minutes or until light. Bake in 425° oven for 20 minutes or until browned and done. (Makes one dozen biscuits.)

BUNKHOUSE BISCUITS

2 c. sifted flour
3 tsp. baking powder
1/2 tsp. salt

4 T. cold shortening
3/4 c. milk

Sift dry ingredients together and mix in shortening. Add milk to make dough. Using a floured board, knead lightly, using a minimum of flour on board. Roll out dough 1/2 inch thick and cut with floured biscuit cutter. Place on greased baking sheet and bake at 450° about 12 minutes.

WYLIE'S OATMEAL MUFFINS

1¼ c. flour
1 T. baking powder
1 tsp. salt
⅓ c. sugar
1 c. uncooked quick rolled
 oats

½ c. raisins
1 egg
1 c. milk
⅓ c. melted fat or oil

Mix flour, baking powder, salt, and sugar in large bowl. Stir in rolled oats and raisins. Beat egg and add milk. Add fat or oil. Add milk mixture to flour mixture. Stir just until dry ingredients are wet, leaving batter lumpy. Fill greased muffin pans half full. Bake at 400° for 20-25 minutes or until muffins are browned. Makes 12 muffins.

MESQUITE SAM'S MUFFINS

1 (15 oz.) Raisin Bran
3 c. sugar
1 qt. buttermilk
5 tsp. soda

1 c. melted shortening
4 eggs, beaten
5 c. flour
2 tsp. salt

Mix bran, sugar, flour, soda, and salt in a **large** mixing bowl. Add eggs, shortening, and buttermilk. Mix well. Store in covered dish in refrigerator until ready to bake. Bake at 400° for 15-20 minutes. (Will keep up to 6 weeks.)

CHISHOLM TRAIL MUFFINS

2 c. flour
3 tsp. baking powder
1/4 c. sugar
1 tsp. salt

1 egg
1 c. milk
1/4 c. salad oil

Heat oven to 400°. Grease 15 muffin cups. Sift all dry ingredients together. Beat egg; stir in milk and oil. Mix in remaining ingredients just until flour is moistened. Batter should be lumpy. Fill muffin cups 2/3 full. Bake 15-20 minutes. **Variations:** You may add 1/2-1 cup applesauce, crushed pineapple, nuts, apricot jam, blueberries, etc. Makes 15 muffins.

SUNDANCE SOURDOUGH MUFFINS

1/2 c. whole-wheat flour
1 1/2 c. white flour
1/2 c. melted shortening
1/2 c. sugar
1/2 c. evaporated milk (do not dilute)

2 eggs
1 c. raisins
1 tsp. salt
1 tsp. soda
1/2 c. sourdough

Stir only enough to blend. Bake in greased muffin pans at 425° for 25 minutes. In place of the canned milk, 1/2 cup water plus 2 tablespoons dry milk can be substituted.

Robert E. Kerby
B/K ©

OLD-FASHIONED BLUEBERRY COBBLER

2 T. cornstarch
1/4 c. brown sugar
1 c. water

3 c. blueberries
1 T. butter
1 T. lemon juice

Topping:

1 c. flour
1/2 c. sugar
1 1/2 tsp. baking powder

1/2 tsp. salt
1/2 c. milk
1/4 c. soft butter

Mix cornstarch, brown sugar, water, and blueberries together. Cook until thickened. Add butter and lemon juice. Pour into baking dish. Mix topping ingredients together and spoon on top. Bake at 350° for 30 minutes. Sprinkle top with nutmeg and sugar.

HOMECOMING TOASTED PIE

Bring to boil:

1 c. milk
1/4 tsp. salt

1/2 c. sugar

Add 3 tablespoons cornstarch dissolved in 1/4 cup water. Cook until smooth, thick, and glossy. Add 1/2 tablespoon plain gelatin dissolved in 1/4 cup water, 1 cup toasted almonds or toasted coconut, and 2 teaspoons vanilla. For meringue, use 4 egg whites. Add 1/4 cup sugar and beat until just stiff. Then gradually add 1/4 cup more sugar and beat until stiff, but not dry. Fold the hot mixture into the meringue. Turn mixture into a baked pie shell. Chill at least 3 hours. Top with whipped cream and either toasted coconut or toasted almonds.

MULESKINNER'S APRICOT PIE

5 c. apricots, halved
3/4 c. sugar
1/4 tsp. nutmeg
1/4 tsp. salt

1 T. flour
1 T. lemon juice
1 T. butter

Topping:

1 T. butter
3 T. flour

1 T. sugar
1/4 tsp. salt

Combine sugar, nutmeg, salt, and flour. Sprinkle lemon juice over apricots. Arrange apricots and dry mixture in alternate layers in an **unbaked** pie shell. Dot with butter. Cover with top crust of unbaked pastry. Crumble topping ingredients and sprinkle over top. Bake at 425° for 10 minutes; reduce heat to 350° and bake for 25 minutes.

COWBOY ARTISTS DELIGHT
(Sour Cream Pecan Pie)

1 unbaked 9-inch pastry shell	2 T. margarine, melted
3 eggs, slightly beaten	1 tsp. vanilla
1/2 c. sour cream	1/8 tsp. salt
1 c. sugar	1 1/4 c. pecan halves
1/2 c. dark corn syrup	

Pierce pastry shell thoroughly with fork. Bake in 400° oven for 8 minutes, or until lightly browned. Cool. In a medium bowl, stir together eggs and sour cream until smooth. Stir in sugar, corn syrup, margarine, vanilla, and salt until well mixed. Stir in pecans. Pour into prebaked pastry shell. Bake in a 400° oven for 30-35 minutes or until filling is slightly puffy, but set, about 1 inch from edge. Cool on wire rack.

SOUTHERN PECAN PIE

Pastry for 9-inch pie shell	1/2 tsp. vanilla
3 eggs	1 c. sugar
1 T. melted butter	1 T. flour
1 c. light corn syrup	1 c. pecan halves

Arrange cup pecan halves in bottom of pie shell. Beat eggs. Add butter, corn syrup, and vanilla. Stir until well blended. Combine sugar and flour and blend with the egg mixture. Pour over nuts. Let stand until nuts rise to the top. Bake at 400° for 10 minutes, then reduce heat to 325° for about 30 minutes.

SHOTGUN RED'S CHERRY PIE

2 c. pitted cherries	1/2 tsp. cinnamon
3/4 c. honey	9-inch unbaked pie shell &
3 T. tapioca	strips
1 T. butter	

Combine cherries, honey, and tapioca. Pour into pie shell. Dot with butter. Sprinkle with cinnamon. Cover with lattice-top crust. Bake in 450° oven for 10 minutes. Reduce heat. Bake in moderate oven (350°) for 30 minutes.

HELL RAISIN' SOUR CREAM RAISIN PIE

1/2 c. raisins	1 c. sugar
1/2 c. water (cook a few minutes until tender)	2 egg yolks
	2 T. cornstarch
1 c. sour cream (either farm or commercial)	1 tsp. vanilla

Blend all this, and add to raisins. Cook until smooth. Put in 8-inch baked shell. Cover with meringue made of 2 egg whites, 4 tablespoons sugar, and about 1/8 teaspoon baking powder. Bake at 325° for 20 minutes or until brown.

HUNGRY DROVER'S OATMEAL PIE

3 eggs, well beaten	2/3 c. quick-cooking oatmeal
2/3 c. white sugar	2/3 c. coconut
1 c. brown sugar	1 tsp. vanilla
2 T. butter	

Blend all ingredients and pour into unbaked pie crust. Bake at 350° for 30-35 minutes. Tastes similar to pecan pie.

AFTER BRANDIN' PUMPKIN PIE

1/2 c. oatmeal	1/2 c. brown sugar
1 c. flour	1/2 c. butter

Mix together and press in 9 x 13-inch pan. Bake 15 minutes at 350°. Mix together:

2 c. pumpkin	1/2 tsp. salt
1 can (13 1/2-oz.) evaporated milk	1/2 tsp. ground ginger
3/4 c. sugar	1 tsp. cinnamon
2 eggs	1/2 tsp. cloves

Pour into crust and bake for 20 minutes at 350°. Mix:

1/2 c. pecans	1/2 c. brown sugar
2 T. butter	

After mixing together, spread on top of pumpkin. Bake for 15-20 minutes longer at 350°.

BRONC BUSTER'S PIE CRUST

3 c. flour
1¼ c. shortening
1 egg, well beaten

5 T. water
1 T. vinegar
Dash of salt

Cut shortening into flour and salt. Combine egg, water, and vinegar. Pour liquid into flour mixture all at once. Blend with spoon just until flour is moistened. This is an easy crust to handle and can be rerolled without toughening. It will keep in the refrigerator up to 2 weeks.

LARAMIE LEMONADE PIE

Blend well 1 small can frozen lemonade and 1 can Eagle Brand milk. Fold into 1 (8-ounce) carton Cool Whip. Pour into a cooked pastry shell or graham cracker crust. Chill.

PALE RIDER PUMPKIN PIE

Mix together:

2 eggs
1½ c. pumpkin
½ tsp. salt
½ tsp. allspice

1 tsp. cinnamon
½ tsp. nutmeg
¾ c. sugar
1½ c. milk

Pour into unbaked pastry shell. Bake in preheated 425° oven for 15 minutes. Reduce heat to 350° and bake for 45 more minutes.

CATTLE DRIVE DUTCH APPLE PIE

6 c. sliced cooking apples
½ c. sugar
1 tsp. cinnamon
1 unbaked 9-inch pie shell

1 c. all-purpose flour
¾ c. firmly-packed brown sugar
½ c. butter or margarine,
  softened

Preheat oven to 400°. In a large bowl, combine apples, sugar, and cinnamon. Toss to coat. Layer apple slices in pie shell. In a small bowl, combine flour and brown sugar. With a pastry blender or two knives, cut in butter or margarine until mixture is crumbly. Sprinkle crumb mixture evenly over apples in pie shell. Bake 50 minutes. Let cool on a wire rack.

GHOST RIDER'S RAPTURE

Mix together:

1 c. flour

1 c. butter or margarine, room temp.

1 c. nuts, chopped

Spread into a 13 x 9 x 2-inch baking dish. Bake 25 minutes at 350⁰. Mix together.

1 c. confectioners' sugar

8 oz. cream cheese, softened

1 c. whipped topping

Spread over nut crust. Mix together:

1 pkg. vanilla instant pudding

1 pkg. chocolate instant pudding

3 c. milk

Spread over cream cheese filling. Top with whipped topping and nuts. The puddings can be mixed together or mixed and spread on one at a time. (Use 1½ cups milk for each pudding.) A pretty effect for a party; marbelize by dropping spoonsful and swirling around.) Yields 12 servings.

COWBOYS' CREAM PUFFS

In a saucepan boil 1 cup water. Add 1 stick margarine and ¼ teaspoon salt. When melted, **quickly** stir in 1 cup flour. Mix well. The dough will form a ball. Remove from heat. Cool for 5 minutes. Add, **one at a time**, 4 eggs. Dough will be smooth and shiny. Mound puffs with a spoon onto a lightly-greased cookie sheet. Place about 2 inches apart. They will triple in size. Bake in a pre-heated 450⁰ oven for 15 minutes. Reduce oven temperature to 325⁰ and bake for 20 minutes more. Remove when done. Turn off oven. Slit puffs about halfway through horizontally. Put back into open oven to dry out 2 or 3 minutes. Place on rack to cool. Store in an airtight container until ready to serve. Yields 12 large or 25-28 miniature. **VARIATIONS: Custard Filling:** Fill cooled puffs with your favorite custard. Top with fudge sauce. **In a Hurry:** Place puff in a bowl. Pour custard or sauce on top. **Party Puffs:** Make miniature puffs. Fill with chicken salad, tuna salad, or any of your favorite meat fillings.

SPOTTED PUP (Rice Pudding)

Take whatever amount needed for hungry cowboys of nice fluffy, cooked rice. Put in Dutch oven and cover with milk and well-beaten eggs. Add sugar to sweeten well, a dash of salt, raisins, and a little nutmeg. Vanilla can be used as flavoring. Bake in slow oven until egg mixture is done and raisins soft. **Plain Pup:** (Same as Spotted Pup but omit the raisins.) When cooking in Dutch oven be sure coals are not too hot. This pudding is best if it never boils. If it boils, eggs and milk curdle.

PAWNEE BREAD PUDDING

1/2 c. sugar	1 tsp. vanilla
1/2 tsp. cinnamon	8 slices bread, cut in cubes
1/4 tsp. salt	1/2 c. seedless raisins
2 eggs	2 T. butter, melted
1 qt. (4 c.) fluid milk	

Mix sugar, cinnamon, and salt in a large bowl. Beat in eggs and slowly stir in milk and vanilla. Stir in bread cubes, raisins, and butter. Pour into 9-inch square pan. Bake at 350° about an hour, or until knife stuck near center comes out clean.

GENERAL CUSTER'S CUSTARD
(Serve on June 25th)

Beat well with a mixer 6 eggs. Add 1 cup sugar and 1/4 teaspoon salt. Scald and add slowly 4 cups milk. Add 1 teaspoon vanilla. Butter 8 oven-proof custard cups. Pour mixture into cups. Place into a pan that has 2 cups hot water in it. Bake in a preheated 425° oven for 10 minutes. Reduce heat and bake at 325° for 30-40 more minutes. Insert blade of knife in middle of custard. When knife comes out clean, custard is done. **Optional:** Sprinkle with nutmeg before baking. Serve either warm or cold.

INDIAN PUDDING DESSERT

4 c. milk	1/2 c. sugar
1/2 c. cornmeal	1/2 tsp. cinnamon
1 tsp. salt	2 T. butter
1/4 c. corn syrup	

Put milk in a saucepan and add cornmeal and salt. Cook for 15 minutes and remove from heat. Add syrup and sugar. Stir in cinnamon and butter. Put into a greased baking dish in 350° oven for 1 1/2-2 hours. Serve warm or cold.

GHOST TOWN DESSERT

In a medium saucepan melt 1 cup butter. Add and stir until dissolved 3 tablespoons cocoa and 2 cups sugar. Remove from heat and add 4 eggs, 1 tablespoon vanilla, 1 cup flour, and 1-2 cups chopped pecans. **Stir as little as possible.** Pour into an 8 x 8 x 2-inch buttered dish. Place this dish into a larger pan that has 1 cup of hot water in it. Place in a preheated 300⁰ oven and bake for 1 hour and 10 minutes. Serve warm or cold. It's delicious either way. **The secret is in the mixing. Stir only to mix.**

END OF THE TRAIL CHOCOLATE CREAM

Melt in medium saucepan 1 package (12-ounce) chocolate chips, 2 tablespoons water, and 1 teaspoon instant coffee. Stir until smooth and remove from heat. Cool. Add 6 egg yolks, one at a time, and beat well after each. In separate bowl, beat 6 egg whites until frothy. Add $1/4$ teaspoon cloves and 2 teaspoons cinnamon. Add and beat until stiff 6 tablespoons sugar. Fold into chocolate mixture. Fold into above mixture 1 large carton whipped topping (reserve small amount). Put into individual serving bowls or glass container. Refrigerate. To serve, top with more whipped topping and serve with plain cookies. (Make the day before you plan to serve.) Yields 6-8 servings.

HAPPY TRAILS GRANOLA

Mix:

6 c. oats	**$1/2$ c. bran**
1 c. wheat germ	**$1/4$ c. sunflower nuts**
1 c. coconut	**1 tsp. nutmeg**
1 c. mixed nuts, chopped	**2 tsp. cinnamon**
$1/4$ c. sesame seeds	

Heat (low heat, briefly):

$1/2$ c. oil	**$1/2$ c. honey**
$1/4$ c. water	**$1/4$ c. molasses**

Combine dry and liquid ingredients and add 1 tablespoon vanilla. Bake at 250⁰, stirring every 10 minutes until done (about 30 minutes total).

Robert E. Korby
B/K ©

MINNEHAHA CAKE (Old Time Recipe)

1/2 c. butter	2 1/2 c. flour
1 1/2 c. sugar	1 tsp. cream of tartar
3 whole eggs	1 tsp. baking soda
1 c. sweet milk	Lemon flavoring

Bake in layers (makes 3) at moderate heat, for 25-30 minutes. To mix, place butter and sugar into bowl; blend with the fingers until creamy. Add eggs and mix (beat eggs beforehand). Dredge flour and cream of tartar and baking soda together. Add a little milk, then a little flour mixture to the butter mixture. Repeat this method until all flour and milk are gone. Stir good. Batter must be smooth and well blended. Flavor. (When Royal Baking Powder came on the market around the turn of the century, 2 tablespoonfuls of baking powder were used instead of the cream of tartar and baking soda. This improved the cake.)

Custard Filling:

1 pt. milk	1 T. cornstarch (dissolved in 1 T. milk)
2 eggs	
1/2 c. sugar	

Let these mixed ingredients boil until thickened and sticks to the spoon. Flavor with vanilla. Set aside to cool while frosting for top of cake is made. When custard is cold, spread between the cold cake layers. **For the frosting:** 1 cup sugar and 4 tablespoons water. Boil until clear. Stir into the beaten white of 1 egg, quickly, and add 1/2 cup raisins. The raisins should be chopped fine. Add 1/2 cup chopped wild hickory nutmeats (walnuts may be used). When quite cool, spread over top and sides of the 3-layer cake.

Robert E. Kerby
8/K

SOUTHWESTERN CAKE

1¾ c. sifted flour	2 eggs, separated
1 tsp. baking soda	1 tsp. vanilla extract
½ tsp. salt	½ c. buttermilk or sour milk
½ c. butter or margarine	1 c. mashed bananas
1 c. brown sugar	½ c. chopped pitted dates
½ c. granulated sugar	½ c. chopped walnuts

Grease and flour a 9-inch square pan. Sift flour with baking soda and salt. Set aside. Cream butter until light and then gradually add the sugars, beating until mixture is light and fluffy. Beat in egg yolks and vanilla. Combine buttermilk or sour milk with mashed bananas. Add the sifted dry ingredients to the creamed mixture alternately with the banana mixture. Blend in dates and nuts. Beat egg whites until stiff and fold them in last. Turn batter into prepared pan and bake in 350° oven for 45 minutes, or until cake tests done. Cool on rack, in the pan. When completely cool, top with favorite frosting.

BRONC BUSTER'S DUMP CAKE

1 (#2) can crushed pineapple	1½ cubes butter
1 (#2) can cherry pie filling	½ c. chopped nuts
1 cake mix (yellow or white)	

Grease a 9 x 13 x 2-inch pan. Dump pineapple over entire bottom. Dump cherry pie filling over pineapple. Shake dry cake mix evenly over the fruit. Slice butter over top and sprinkle nuts over all. Bake 1 hour at 350°. Serve from baking pan and top with whipped cream or ice cream.

Robert E. Roaby
B/K

FEED BAG OATMEAL CAKE

1 c. quick oats
1 1/4 c. boiling water
1 cube oleo
1 c. white sugar
1 c. brown sugar
2 eggs

1 1/3 c. flour
1 tsp. soda
1 tsp. cinnamon
1/2 tsp. salt
1/4 tsp. nutmeg

Pour the water over the oats and the oleo and let stand 20 minutes. Add the white and brown sugar and eggs. Sift the flour, soda, cinnamon, nutmeg, and salt. Add to oats and bake 35 minutes at 350° in 13 x 9 1/2-inch pan.

Topping:

6 T. butter
1 c. pecans
1 c. coconut

1 1/2 tsp. vanilla
1/2 c. sugar
1/4 c. Pet milk

Mix and spread on warm cake. Put under broiler until brown.

APPLE CAKE DESSERT

4 c. diced apples
2 eggs
2 tsp. cinnamon
1 tsp. baking soda

2 c. sugar, depends on tartness
    of apples
2 c. all-purpose flour, unsifted

Mix apples, sugar, and eggs. Add dry ingredients which have been sifted together. Put in greased 9 x 13-inch pan and bake at 350° for 35-40 minutes.

Topping:

1/2 c. brown sugar
1 c. water

1/2 c. granulated sugar
2 T. flour

Cook until thick and bubbly, about 5 minutes. Remove from heat and add:

1/2 c. margarine   1 tsp. vanilla

Blend with electric mixer. While cake is still warm, poke holes over entire surface with a fork. (Make plenty so topping soaks into cake.) Pour topping over cake. Serve slightly warm or add whipped topping or ice cream.

PRESCOTT ARIZONA FRUITCAKE

4 c. raisins
2 c. orange juice
1 c. butter
2 c. orange marmalade
1 tsp. grated lemon rind
1 T. grated orange rind
1 tsp. baking soda
½ c. orange juice
4 c. sifted flour

1 tsp. nutmeg
1 tsp. allspice
2 tsp. cinnamon
½ tsp. salt
3 eggs
2 c. pitted, chopped dates
2 c. chopped walnuts
1 lb. candied fruit mix

Grease a 10-inch tube pan. Line it with waxed paper and grease the paper. In a large saucepan combine raisins, 2 cups orange juice, and butter. Place over direct heat and bring to a boil, stirring occasionally. Reduce heat and simmer for 10 minutes. Remove from heat and cool. When mixture is cooled, stir in marmalade and grated rind. Dissolve baking soda in the ½ cup orange juice and add to mixture. If the saucepan is large enough, you may mix everything in the pan. If not, turn mixture into a large bowl. Sift together flour, spices, and salt; stir into the mixture along with the remaining ingredients. Mix well with a large wooden spoon or clean hands. Turn batter into prepared pan and bake in 300° oven 3-3½ hours, or until cake tests done. Cool in the pan. When cake is thoroughly cooled, remove pan and then carefully remove the paper. Wrap the cake in cheesecloth and then seal in plastic wrap or plastic storage bag. Age cake at least 4 weeks in a cool, dry place before serving.

HOP-A-LONG CASSIDY'S CAKE

2 c. sugar
½ c. oil
½ c. milk
1 tsp. vanilla
¼ c. cocoa
2 eggs

1 c. water
2 c. flour
2 tsp. vinegar
½ c. oleo
1 tsp. soda

Mix flour and sugar and set aside. Bring oleo, water, oil, and cocoa to a boil, then pour over flour and sugar. Mix well. Combine and mix well the milk, vinegar, vanilla, soda, and eggs. Pour into batter and mix well. Bake 20 minutes at 350° on a cookie sheet with high sides.

Frosting:

1 stick oleo
¼ c. cocoa

5 T. milk
1 tsp. vanilla

Bring to a boil and stir in 1 pound powdered sugar.

TRAIL DRIVER'S STRAWBERRY SHORTCAKE

1 c. small marshmallows (may use more)
2 c. frozen strawberries, thawed
1 (3-oz.) pkg. strawberry Jello
2¼ c. flour
1½ c. sugar
½ c. shortening
3 tsp. baking powder
½ tsp. salt
3 eggs
1 c. milk
1 tsp. vanilla

Grease a 9 x 13-inch pan. Put marshmallows on bottom of pan. Combine strawberries and Jello; set aside. Combine remaining ingredients and beat well. Pour batter over marshmallows; spoon strawberry mixture over batter. Bake for 45 minutes at 350⁰. Top with whipped cream to serve.

CLEARWATER CHEESECAKE

1 (8 oz.) cream cheese, softened
½ c. sugar
1 (4-oz.) carton Cool Whip, thawed
Maraschino cherries
1 tsp. vanilla
½ c. sour cream
Graham cracker crust

Beat cheese until smooth. Gradually beat in sugar. Blend in sour cream and vanilla. Fold in Cool Whip thoroughly. Spoon into a graham cracker crust. Chill about 4 hours. Serve topped with cherries if desired. Serves 6-8.

CRAZY HORSE CHOCOLATE CAKE

Sift the following ingredients into a greased 9 x 13-inch pan.

3 c. flour
2 c. sugar
2 tsp. baking soda
1 c. salad oil
2 tsp. vinegar
1 tsp. salt
6 T. cocoa
2 tsp. vanilla

Add 2 cups cold water and mix well with a fork. If you desire, the recipe ingredients may be first mixed in a bowl before putting in a pan. Bake in 350⁰ oven for 40 minutes.

BANK ROBBER'S $25,000.00 CAKE

Mix well:

1 box German chocolate cake mix, dry	2 eggs, well beaten
	1 tsp. almond flavoring

Batter will be very thick. Grease and flour a 13 x 9 x 2-inch oblong baking dish. Spread mixture evenly in bottom of pan. Carefully spoon over batter 1 can cherry pie filling. Bake in a preheated 350⁰ oven for 25 minutes. Remove from oven and spread frosting on while cake is hot.

Frosting: (Combine in a small saucepan)

$1/3$ c. milk	5 T. butter or margarine
1 c. sugar	

Bring to a boil. Cook 1 minute. Remove from heat and add 6 ounces milk chocolate chips. Stir and frost cake in pan.

GOLD RUSH PINEAPPLE UPSIDE-DOWN CAKE

Melt in the bottom of a large (12-inch) iron skillet 1 cup brown sugar, 1 stick butter, and 1 teaspoon vanilla. Drain. Reserve juice and add 1 (16-ounce) can crushed pineapple. Boil about 5 minutes. In a mixing bowl, cream together $1 1/2$ cups sugar, and 1 stick butter. Add 2 eggs, 1 cup pineapple juice (add water to make full cup), 1 teaspoon vanilla, $2 1/4$ cups flour, $1/2$ teaspoon salt, $1/2$ teaspoon soda, and 1 teaspoon baking powder. Mix well and spread over the pineapple mixture. Bake in preheated 350⁰ oven for 1 hour. When done, let set about 10 minutes before inverting onto serving plate.

Robert E. Kerby
B/K

PAWNEE BILL'S PUMPKIN CAKE

Cream together:

2 c. sugar

4 eggs

Add:

2 c. flour
1 tsp. salt
1 1/2 c. Wesson oil

1 c. pumpkin
2 tsp. soda
3 tsp. cinnamon

Bake in a greased and floured tube pan in a preheated 325° oven for 1 hour. When cool, frost with frosting.

Frosting: (Mix together)

1 stick butter, room temp.
1 box powdered sugar
1 pkg. (3-oz.) cream cheese

1 T. vanilla
1 c. pecans, chopped

Spread mixture on cooled cake.

FIXIN' FENCE FROSTING

1/4 c. butter, softened
2 c. sifted confectioner's sugar
3 T. milk

1 tsp. vanilla extract
Dash of salt
1/2 c. peanut butter

In small saucepan heat butter over low heat, stirring occasionally until butter turns light amber. Beat in sugar, milk, vanilla, and salt. Stir in peanut butter.

Robert E. Kirby
B/K

2 level tsp. soda
1/2 tsp. ground cloves

...dients together 6 times. Put in a mixing bowl and ...acle Whip and 1 cup cold coffee. Mix all together, ...r 2 or 3 minutes with the electric mixer. Put in a ...t pan and bake 30 minutes in a 350⁰ oven. The batter will ...y thin.

Chocolate Frosting:

6 oz. semi-sweet chocolate
  pieces
1/2 c. evaporated milk

2 1/2 c. sifted confectioners'
  sugar

Melt chocolate pieces with evaporated milk in heavy 1-quart saucepan over very low heat or in mixing bowl in microwave. Stir in sugar until smooth. If frosting becomes too thick to spread easily, add a few more drops of evaporated milk.

BUNKHOUSE HOMEMADE ICE CREAM

Separate into two bowls 6 eggs. Add to egg whites and beat until very fluffy 1 cup sugar. Set aside. Add to egg yolks and beat until fluffy 1 cup sugar. Set aside. Beat until stiff 2 cups heavy cream. Blend all mixtures together and add 2 teaspoons vanilla. Pour into prechilled freezer can. Finish filling with milk or half and half cream. Freeze according to manufacturer's manual. Try this once! You will never make ice cream any other way. Yields 1 gallon.

COLD TRAIL ICE CREAM

6 eggs, beaten
2 c. sugar
1 can Eagle Brand milk
1 pt. whipping cream

1 qt. half & half
3-4 T. vanilla
Pinch of salt

Add sugar to beaten eggs. Mix. Add Eagle Brand, whipping cream, and half and half. Then add vanilla and a pinch of salt. Add milk to the fill line. Freeze.

CHUCKWAGON CHARLIE'S CHOCOLATE SAUCE

Stir over low heat for 2 minutes 1 cup sugar and 2 tablespoons cocoa. Then add 7/8 cup evaporated milk and 2 tablespoons butter. Stir constantly. Bring to a rapid boil. Boil for 1 minute. Serve warm or cold. Excellent on ice cream, pound cake, etc.

BROWN SAGE BROWNIES

Melt in a medium saucepan:

1 stick margarine	3 heaping T. cocoa

Add:

1 c. sugar	1/4 tsp. salt
1 c. flour	1 tsp. vanilla
2 eggs	Pecans

Mix by hand, only enough to moisten. Bake in a well-greased and floured oblong pan at 375° for 20-30 minutes. Do not overbake. When done, pour on Chocolate Icing while brownies are still hot. Let cool. Cut into squares.

Chocolate Icing: (bring to boil)

1/4 c. margarine	3 T. milk
2 level T. cocoa	

Boil 1 minute. Remove from heat and add 1/2 box powdered sugar and 1 teaspoon vanilla. Pour over hot brownies. **VARIATION: Peanut Butter Brownies:** Add 1 small package peanut butter chips to brownie mixture.

ROCKY MOUNTAIN BROWNIES

3/4 c. butter	3/4 tsp. baking soda
3/4 c. sugar	1/4 tsp. salt
2 eggs	1 c. plain chocolate candies
1 tsp. vanilla	3/4 c. coarsely-chopped nuts
1 1/2 c. flour	1/2 c. raisins
1/4 c. cocoa powder	2/3 c. miniature marshmallows

Beat together butter and sugar until light and fluffy; blend in eggs and vanilla. Add combined flour, cocoa, soda, and salt; mix well. Stir in 1/2 cup candies, 1/2 cup nuts, and raisins. Spread batter into greased 13 x 9-inch baking pan. Sprinkle with remaining 1/2 cup candies and 1/4 cup nuts. Bake at 350° for 15 minutes. Sprinkle marshmallows over partially baked bars, pressing in lightly. Continue baking about 15 minutes or until edges are set. (Do not overbake.) Cool thoroughly; cut into bars. Makes 1 (13 x 9-inch) pan of bars.

PEANUT BAR
(Also the Name of a Beer Joint in Georgia)

1/2 c. peanut butter (chunky)　　　1/2 c. dry milk powder
1/2 c. honey

Heat peanut butter in a double boiler until it is a thick soup. Stir in the honey and then the dry milk. Mix well and remove from heat. Pack into cupcake papers. (1.) Refrigerate bars, then coat with semi-sweet or dipping chocolate. (2.) Mix shredded coconut in the chocolate before dipping. (Makes 6 quarter-cup or 3 half-cup bars.)

IRON BARS (A Jailer's Favorite)

1/3 c. butter or margarine　　　　1/4 c. toasted wheat germ
1 c. dark raisins　　　　　　　　1 1/2 tsp. baking powder
1/2 c. golden raisins　　　　　　1/2 tsp. baking soda
1/2 c. sugar　　　　　　　　　　1 c. sliced almonds
1/2 c. golden molasses　　　　　1/2 c. liquid milk
1 egg　　　　　　　　　　　　　1 c. quick-cooking rolled oats
1 1/4 c. whole-wheat flour　　　　1/2 tsp. salt
1/4 c. nonfat dry milk　　　　　　1/2 tsp. ginger

Chop raisins. Cream butter, sugar, and molasses together. Combine whole-wheat flour, nonfat dry milk, wheat germ, baking powder, soda, salt, and ginger and mix lightly. Blend into creamed mixture alternately with liquid milk. Stir in oats, raisins, and half of the almonds. Turn into greased baking pan (9 x 12 inches) and spread evenly. Sprinkle with remaining half cup of almonds. Bake in moderate oven (350º) about 30 minutes until cookies test done. Cool in pan, then cut into bars.

ANGUS CHOCOLATE CLUSTERS

1 (6-oz.) pkg. (1 c.) semi-sweet　　1 c. flaked or shredded coconut
　chocolate pieces　　　　　　　2 c. rolled oats (quick or
1/3 c. butter　　　　　　　　　　　old-fashioned)
16 lg. marshmallows

Melt chocolate pieces, butter, or marshmallows over low heat or in microwave. Stir until smooth. Remove from heat or microwave. Stir in coconut and oats. Mix thoroughly. Drop from teaspoon onto waxed paper. Refrigerate. Yields 3 dozen.

SIERRA COOKIES

Combine the following in a large bowl, then mix at medium speed:

1 c. shortening	1 c. brown sugar (packed)
2 T. vanilla	2 tsp. nutmeg
1 tsp. cinnamon	2 eggs
2/3 c. milk	

Then add following and mix at slow speed:

2 c. flour	1 tsp. soda
1 tsp. salt	

Clean off beaters and hand mix the following:

1/2 jar glazed fruit	1/2 box raisins
1/2 pkg. sliced walnuts	

Mix thoroughly, then blend in by hand 4 cups of oatmeal. Press down in a greased 12 x 18-inch cookie pan with the back of a wet spoon. Bake in a 350º oven for 20 minutes. Cut into 24 pieces and wrap in aluminum foil or put in plastic bags. (If they're not to be eaten within a few weeks, keep in freezer to prevent mold from forming.)

DEW DROP INN GUMDROP COOKIES

2 T. water	1/4 tsp. salt
4 eggs	1 tsp. cinnamon
2 c. brown sugar	1 c. gumdrops
2 c. flour	3/4 c. walnuts

Add water to eggs and beat until fluffy. Add sugar and mix well. Sift flour, salt, and cinnamon, and add. Stir in gumdrops and nutmeats and pour into greased 9 x 13-inch pan. Bake in moderate oven 25 minutes. Frost with white icing. Sprinkle with mixed "decors" for a festive look.

OLD SORRELY'S OATMEAL COOKIES

1 c. all-purpose flour
1/2 tsp. salt
1/2 tsp. baking powder
1/2 tsp. baking soda
1/2 c. butter
1/2 c. brown sugar, firmly
  packed

1/2 c. white sugar
1 egg
1 T. water
1 tsp. vanilla
11/2 c. rolled oats
1/2 c. chopped nuts

Mix flour, salt, baking powder, and baking soda together. Cream together butter and sugars. Add egg and continue beating until fluffy. Add water and vanilla, then rolled oats and flour mixture, a little at a time. Fold in coarsely-chopped nuts. Drop by teaspoonfuls onto a greased baking sheet and bake 10-12 minutes at 350° until a light brown.

SILVER BULLET SUGAR COOKIES

1 c. shortening (1/2 butter, 1/2
  oleo)
1 c. sugar
1 egg, unbeaten

21/4 c. flour
1/2 tsp. soda
Pinch of salt
1 tsp. vanilla

Cream sugar and butter. Add egg. Mix dry ingredients and vanilla. Stir well. Make into balls and roll in sugar and flatten with glass. Press a piece of walnut or pecan in the top. Bake at 350° for 8 minutes.

OUT-OF-THE-GATE NO-BAKE COOKIES

1 egg, beaten
1 c. sugar
1 stick oleo
1/8 tsp. salt

1 c. chopped dates
1/2 c. pecans
3 c. Rice Krispies

Cook all ingredients except Rice Krispies in a heavy saucepan until it comes to a boil. Don't boil or overcook. Add Rice Krispies. Form into balls and roll in coconut.

ALBUQUERQUE AL'S APRICOT BARS

1 c. brown sugar, packed
1 c. butter
1 egg
1 tsp. vanilla

13/4 c. flour
1 c. chopped nuts
1/2 c. apricot jam

Beat together sugar, butter, egg, and vanilla until smooth and creamy. Stir in flour and nuts. Spoon 1/2 batter in a greased 9-inch square pan. Spread evenly. Spread batter with jam. Cover jam with remaining batter. Bake in 325° oven for 50 minutes. Cool 10 minutes. Cut into squares. Makes about 32 bars.

KIT CARSON BROWNIE BARS

1/2 c. margarine
3/4 c. sugar
2 eggs
1 tsp. vanilla

3/4 c. flour
2 T. cocoa
1/4 tsp. baking powder
1/4 tsp. salt

Cream margarine and sugar. Add eggs and vanilla. Stir in remaining ingredients. Spread in well-greased 9 x 13-inch pan. Bake at 350° for 15 minutes. Top with 2 cups miniature marshmallows and return to oven for 3 minutes. Cool, then top with the following mixture: Melt 1 (6-ounce) package chocolate chips and 1 cup peanut butter. Stir in 1 1/2 cups Rice Krispies and spread over brownies.

SADDLEPACK COOKIES

1/3 c. butter
1/3 c. brown sugar
1 c. flour
1/2 c. chopped nuts
1/4 c. granulated sugar
1 (8-oz.) pkg. cream cheese,
   softened

1 egg
2 T. milk
1 T. lemon juice
1/2 tsp. vanilla

Cream butter and brown sugar until fluffy. Add flour and nuts and blend until pebbly. Set aside 1 cup of mixture. Press remainder into 8-inch square pan and bake at 350° for 12-15 minutes. Beat sugar and cream cheese together until smooth. Add remaining ingredients and beat. Pour over baked crust; sprinkle with the 1 cup reserved crumbs. Bake for another 25-30 minutes. Cool and cut into 16 bars.

CAMP COOK SUGAR COOKIES

1 c. butter or margarine
1 1/2 c. sugar
3 eggs
1 tsp. vanilla

3 1/2 c. sifted enriched flour
2 tsp. cream of tartar
1 tsp. soda
1/2 tsp. salt

Cream butter or margarine. Add sugar gradually, creaming until light and fluffy. Add eggs, one at a time, beating well. Stir in vanilla. Sift dry ingredients together. Add to creamed mixture. Chill overnight or longer. Roll out; cut in desired shapes. Bake in 350° oven until lightly browned around edges - 12-15 minutes. These cookies freeze well.

PANHANDLE PUMPKIN COOKIES

1/2 c. butter	1 1/2 c. flour
3/4 c. sugar	2 tsp. baking powder
3/4 c. mashed cooked pumpkin	1 tsp. cinnamon
or winter squash	1/2 tsp. salt
2 eggs	1/2 c. raisins, opt.

Preheat oven to 375°. Cream butter and sugar together; beat well. Add pumpkin and eggs. Mix all remaining ingredients in a separate bowl and add to pumpkin mixture. Drop batter by spoonfuls onto greased cookie sheet. Bake for 15 minutes or until light brown. May be frosted to look like a pumpkin.

TEXAS RANGER COOKIES

Cream:

1 c. shortening	1 c. brown sugar
1 c. sugar	

Add:

2 eggs

Stir in:

2 c. flour	2 c. oatmeal, uncooked
1 tsp. baking soda	2 c. Rice Krispies
1/2 tsp. baking powder	1 c. coconut
1/4 tsp. salt	1 tsp. vanilla

Mix well. Mold with hands into balls the size of walnuts. Press flat with a fork. Bake in a preheated 350° oven for 12-14 minutes. (May substitute 2 1/2 cups cornflakes for 2 cups Rice Krispies.

WILD BILL'S WHISKEY BISCUITS
(A Delicious Holiday Treat)

Cream together in a large mixing bowl 1 stick softened butter and 1 cup packed brown sugar. Add 4 slightly-beaten eggs. Mix until dissolved and add to sugar mixture 3 teaspoons soda, and 3 tablespoons buttermilk. Stir in 1/2 cup whiskey (may use orange juice). In a large bowl put 3 cups flour. Stir into flour following:

1 tsp. cloves	1 lb. candied cherries
1 tsp. cinnamon	1 lb. candied pineapple
1 tsp. allspice	2 lbs. pecans
1/2 box white raisins (may use	
cut-up dates)	

Combine flour with creamed mixture. Drop by teaspoonsfuls on cookie sheet, 2 inches apart. Bake in a preheated 375° oven for 8-10 minutes. **Do not get too brown.** Cookies should be slightly soft. Store in an airtight container. Will freeze well. Yields 12 dozen.

CHUCKHOLE CHARLIE'S CHOCOLATE PEANUT COOKIES

Chocolate Dough:

1 c. flour
3/4 c. sugar
1 tsp. salt
1/2 c. shortening

1 egg
2 (1-oz.) env. premelted
    unsweetened chocolate
1 tsp. vanilla extract

Peanut Butter Dough:

2 T. flour
1/2 c. firmly-packed brown sugar

1/4 c. creamy peanut butter
2 T. butter, softened

In large mixer bowl, combine all ingredients for Chocolate Dough. Blend well with mixer. Set aside. In small mixer bowl combine all ingredients for Peanut Butter Dough. Blend well with mixer. Spoon level teaspoon of Chocolate Dough and then a scant 1/2 teaspoon of Peanut Butter Dough. Drop onto ungreased cookie sheets. Press with a fork dipped in flour. Bake at 325° for 12-15 minutes. Cool 1 minute. Remove from cookie sheet. Cookie is very tender. Makes 36-42 cookies.

MAPLE MEMORY COOKIES

2¼ c. flour
2 tsp. baking powder
1/2 tsp. soda
1/2 tsp. salt
1/2 c. firmly-packed brown sugar

3/4 c. shortening
1 egg
1/2 c. maple syrup
1 tsp. maple flavoring
1/2 c. chopped walnuts

In large mixer bowl combine all ingredients except walnuts. Blend well with mixer. Stir in walnuts; mix thoroughly. Drop by rounded teaspoon onto ungreased cookie sheets. If desired, top each with a walnut half. Bake at 400° for 8-10 minutes. Cool. Makes 36-42 cookies. **High Altitude Adjustment (5200 feet)**: Decrease baking powder to 1 teaspoon.

OLD SETTLER OATMEAL CHIP COOKIES

2 c. all-purpose flour
1 tsp. salt
1 tsp. soda
1 c. sugar
1 c. firmly-packed brown sugar
1/2 c. butter, softened

2 eggs
2 c. quick-cooking rolled oats
1 c. chopped almonds
1 c. (6-oz.) pkg. semi-sweet
    chocolate pieces

In large mixer bowl combine all ingredients except oats, almonds, and chocolate pieces. Blend well with mixer. Stir in remaining ingredients; mix thoroughly. If desired, chill dough for easier handling. Shape into balls, using a rounded teaspoon for each. Place on ungreased cookie sheets. Bake at 375° for 10-12 minutes. Cool.

GUNSMOKE GINGERSNAPS

3/4 c. shortening
1 c. brown sugar
1/4 c. molasses
1 egg
2 1/4 c. sifted enriched flour

2 tsp. soda
1/2 tsp. salt
1 tsp. ginger
1 tsp. cinnamon
1/2 tsp. cloves

Cream together first 4 ingredients until fluffy. Sift together dry ingredients; stir into molasses mixture. Form in small balls. Roll in granulated sugar and place 2 inches apart on greased cookie sheet. Bake in moderate oven (375°) about 10 minutes. Cool slightly; remove from pan. Makes about 5 dozen.

GREAT PLAINS OATMEAL CRISPS

1 c. shortening
1 c. brown sugar
1 c. granulated sugar
2 eggs
1 tsp. vanilla
1 1/2 c. sifted enriched flour

1 tsp. salt
1 tsp. soda
3 c. quick-cooking rolled oats
1/2 c. chopped California
    walnuts

Thoroughly cream shortening and sugars. Add eggs and vanilla. Beat well. Sift together flour, salt, and soda; add to creamed mixture. Stir in rolled oats and nuts. Mix well. Form dough in rolls, 1-1 1/2 inches in diameter. Wrap in waxed paper, aluminum foil, or Saran wrapping. Chill thoroughly. With sharp knife, slice cookies about 1/4 inch thick. Bake on ungreased cookie sheet in moderate oven (350°) 10 minutes or until lightly browned. Makes about 5 dozen.

BRANDING TIME PEANUT BUTTER COOKIES

1 c. vegetable oil or melted
  margarine
2/3 c. peanut butter
1 c. brown sugar
1 c. white sugar

2 eggs
3 c. flour
2 tsp. soda
1 tsp. salt
1 tsp. vanilla

Mix all ingredients together and form in small balls and press down with a fork. Bake at 350º for 12 minutes. Do not grease the pan. Makes 3 1/2 dozen.

SHERIFF'S POSSE SNICKERDOODLES

1 c. soft shortening (part butter)
1 1/2 c. sugar
2 eggs
2 3/4 c. flour
2 tsp. cream of tartar

1 tsp. soda
1/4 tsp. salt
2 T. sugar
2 tsp. cinnamon

Heat oven to 400º. Mix shortening, sugar, and eggs thoroughly. Mix flour, cream of tartar, soda, and salt. Stir all together. Form into balls the size of small walnuts. Combine sugar and cinnamon and roll balls in this mixture. Place balls about 2 inches apart on ungreased baking sheet. Bake 8-10 minutes. Makes about 6 dozen cookies.

BELLE STARR'S SUGAR COOKIES

3 c. flour
1 tsp. cream of tartar
1 tsp. baking soda
1/2 tsp. salt

1 c. Imperial margarine (may
  use 1/2 shortening)2 eggs
1 c. sugar
1 tsp. vanilla

Combine all dry ingredients in a bowl. Set aside. Cream margarine, vanilla, and sugar. Add eggs, one at a time, beating well after each. Stir in flour mixture. Roll into small balls; place on lightly-greased cookie sheet. Flatten with a glass which you press into sugar (may use colored sugar). Bake at 375º for 8-10 minutes. Yields about 4 dozen.

OLD TIME POPCORN BALLS

Boil together 1 cup white Karo and 1/2 cup sugar. When sugar is melted, remove from heat and add 1 package (3-ounce) Jello (any flavor). Mix well and pour over 2-5 quarts popped popcorn. Stir in with wooden spoon. Grease hands with butter and form into balls. Be very careful not to burn hands.

CACTUS JACK'S CANDY

Select prickly pear cactus (or small barrel cactus if you own this type of cactus, since it's illegal to remove it from the dessert). Remove spines and outside layer with large knife. Cut pulp across in slices 1-inch thick. Soak overnight in cold water. Remove from water. Cut in 1-inch cubes and cook in boiling water until tender. Drain. Cook slowly in the following syrup until nearly all the syrup is absorbed. Do not scorch!

Syrup for 2 quarts of Cactus Cubes:

3 c. granulated sugar	2 T. orange juice
1 c. water	1 T. lemon juice

Heat all ingredients until sugar is dissolved, then add cactus. Remove cactus from syrup; drain and roll in granulated or powdered sugar. For colored cactus candy, any vegetable coloring may be added to the syrup.

TOM MIX TAFFY

Combine in saucepan:

2 c. sugar	1/2 c. vinegar
1 c. water	

Cook to 265° on candy thermometer (hard ball stage). Pour onto buttered pans. Let cool enough to handle. Pull and stretch (with buttered hands) until almost white. Let taffy get completely hard. Break or cut into bite-sized pieces.

JIM BOB'S PEANUT BRITTLE

Use a cast-iron skillet or a heavy saucepan. Bring to a fast boil on high heat:

2 c. sugar	1/2 c. water
3/4 c. light Karo	

Stir as little as possible. Using a wooden spoon, dip into syrup. Hold over pan and allow to drizzle off spoon. When it spins a thread 4-6 inches, add 1 package (12-ounce) raw peanuts. Reduce heat to medium and cook until a golden brown (not dark). Remove from heat and add a dash of salt, 1 teaspoon vanilla, and 1 tablespoon butter. Mix well. Add 2 teaspoons baking soda. **Mix quickly** only until mixture looks milky. Pour immediately onto ungreased cookie sheets. Cool and break into pieces.

SANTA FE PRALINES

Combine in a heavy saucepan and bring to a boil:

2½ c. sugar	2 T. butter
2 T. Karo	⅔ c. evaporated milk

Cook on high to 238° on candy thermometer (soft ball). Remove from heat and beat until creamy. Add 1 ½-2 cups pecans. Drop by teaspoon onto waxed paper.

MICRO PRALINES

Combine in a 3-quart casserole:

1½ c. light brown sugar, firmly packed	⅔ c. half & half cream
	⅛ tsp. salt

Mix well and stir in 2 tablespoons butter. Microwave on high (100% power) for 7-9 minutes, to softball stage. Stir once while cooking. Add 1½ cups pecan halves. Cook 1 more minute. Beat until creamy, about 3 minutes. Drop by teaspoonfuls on waxed paper.

HORSETRADER P.P.G (Peanut Pattie Candy)

Combine in a very heavy saucepan:

3 c. raw peanuts	2½ c. sugar
1 c. milk	⅔ c. white Karo

Cook 1 hour and 10 minutes over low heat. Then add 1 tablespoon butter, 1 teaspoon vanilla, and red cake coloring. Hand beat until cool. Pour out on waxed paper. Cool and break into pieces (or drop into patties with tablespoon).

CIRCUIT JUDGE'S CARAMEL CANDY

In a heavy saucepan melt 1 cup butter. Add and cook over medium heat 1 box (1 pound) brown sugar and a dash of salt. Stir well. Blend in 1 cup light Karo and 1 can Eagle Brand milk. Cook and stir until candy reaches the firm ball stage (245-248° on candy thermometer). Remove from heat. Add 1 teaspoon vanilla and 2 cup pecans. Pour into a buttered 9 x 9 x 2-inch baking dish and cool. Cut into 1-inch squares and wrap in pieces of Saran Wrap.

WILDHORSE WHITE FUDGE

Combine and cook on medium high 2 cups sugar, 1 carton sour cream, and a dash of salt. Stir only occasionally. Cook to 238° on candy thermometer (soft ball). Add 1 tablespoon vanilla, 2 tablespoons butter, and ½-1 cup chopped pecans. Beat until mixture thickens. Pour into a buttered dish. Cut into squares when almost cool.

PISTOL PACKIN' PEANUT BUTTER FUDGE

Mix in a heavy saucepan 2 cups sugar, 1 tablespoon light Karo, $2/3$ cup milk, and 2 tablespoons butter. Cook to softball stage (234-238° on candy thermometer). Remove from heat and add 1 cup peanut butter, 1 teaspoon vanilla and a dash of salt. Blend. Pour quickly into a buttered dish. Cool 10 minutes and cut into squares.

WILD GAME

BUFFALO BILL'S SWEET-SOUR WILD MEAT

This basic recipe may be used for any wild meat. It takes the wild flavor out and leaves a tender, wonderful meal. If meat is sliced, steaks, chops, etc., brown each piece in olive oil. If meat is in shape of roast, brown in olive oil. If steaks, layer pieces with this sauce in between layers; if roast, coat roast with this sauce and baste frequently while cooking.

1 1/2 tsp. salt
1/2 c. brown sugar
2 tsp. mustard

2 T. vinegar
6 T. olive oil

Allowing 20 minutes to the pound, add 1 cup water. Cover and cook at 400°. A large onion cut in half crosswise and placed in either end of pan greatly improves flavor. For gravy, thicken with flour.

FIRESIDE DEER BURGERS

3 lbs. ground deer meat
2 cloves garlic, minced
1 c. wine
1 tsp. salt & pepper

1 onion, chopped
2 T. parsley flakes
2 T. Worcestershire sauce
1 T. sage

Combine all ingredients and mix them thoroughly, then shape the mixture into burger patties. Cook burgers on an outdoor grill over medium heat.

OLD WEST VENISON STEW

1 1/2 lbs. venison stew
2 c. chopped onions
1 c. chopped green peppers
1 c. sliced carrots

1/2 c. chopped celery
4 med. potatoes, cubed
Salt & black pepper

Cut meat into 1 to 1-1/2 inch cubes. Pepper and dredge meat in flour. Heat 1 inch deep oil in heavy skillet and brown meat well on all sides. Put browned meat into stew pot. Add ingredients. Cover with water; simmer over low heat until meat is tender. Add 2 cups water to hot skillet. Scrape brownings off bottom. Thicken broth with flour; add to stew. Boil and add salt 5 minutes before serving.

TRAIL BOSS'S STRING BEANS AND VENISON

2 lbs. deer shoulder, cut into pieces
2 lg. onions, chopped
2 lbs. French-cut string beans
Salt & pepper to taste
1/4 c. margarine
1 T. tomato paste
1 can stewed tomatoes, diced
1 c. water

Place chopped onion in margarine. Cook until onions are clarified. Season meat and brown slightly. Add stewed tomatoes and simmer until meat is about half-cooked. Add string beans, salt, pepper, and tomato paste mixed in water. Stir well and continue simmering until meat and beans are tender. Do not stir too often or beans will fall apart. Serve on a large platter with beans on bottom and meat pieces on top.

TUCCUMCARI TURTLE

Cut the meat loose from the shell. Gut and cut into pieces about 3 inches in diameter and 1 inch thick, or into chunks. Soak the meat overnight in salt water with a pinch of soda added to remove the wild taste. Parboil, if desired, and roll in flour with salt and pepper to taste. Fry the meat in hot lard in a covered skillet until brown on all sides.

GIDDY UP TURTLE SOUP

To prepare the meat:

2 or 3-lb. turtle, cleaned
1/2 lb. lean pork
1/2 tsp. salt
1/2 tsp. coarsely-ground pepper
2 bay leaves
1/2 tsp. cumin

Place the meat and seasoning in pan. Cover with water and simmer until the meat is tender. Remove the meat and chop it fine or cut into cubes. Strain off liquid and set it aside for stock.

To make soup:

3 c. chopped turtle and pork
1 (#303) can stewed tomatoes
2 med. potatoes, diced
4 carrots, sliced
1 T. pimento

Mix all the ingredients in a large pan. Cover with turtle stock and simmer until the vegetables are done. Salt and pepper to taste.

RODEO OPOSSUM CASSEROLE

1-2 lb. 'possum (dressed
  weight)
2 red pepper pods
Flour

5 or 6 c. water
Salt & pepper
4 sweet potatoes, halved

Start oven and set at 350°. Carefully remove scent glands and any clinging hair. Wash very well. Put in pan; cover with water. Add salt and pepper and 1 pod. Put lid on and boil until meat just starts to separate from bone. This will take about 1 1/2 hours. Drain, and discard broth. Put 'possum in baking pan, and sprinkle with flour. Put a peeled potato inside of 'possum and place the rest of them around it. Add 1 cup water. Crush other red pepper pod and place over 'possum and potatoes. Bake, covered, until potatoes are done and meat is tender. For the last 1/2 hour, remove the lid so it can brown. This is best when served hot.

BILLY BOB'S FRIED MUSKRAT

Wash and cut into pieces; soak in salt water for 1 hour. Rinse and dry. Dip pieces in prepared egg batter. Dust with flour and brown in greased frying pan. When brown, fry slowly 1 hour. Make milk gravy in same pan and pour over meat to serve.

BACKWOODS COON BURGERS

2 lbs. ground coon meat,
  racoon if you're a Yankee
1 c. cornbread crumbs
1 egg, beaten
1/2 tsp. salt
1/2 c. catsup
1/4 c. cooking oil

1 onion, minced
2 stalks celery, minced
1/4 tsp. black pepper
1/8 tsp. cayenne pepper
1 tsp. Worcestershire
1 tsp. sage

Combine and thoroughly mix the meat, bread crumbs, egg, salt, pepper, sage, onion, and celery together. Then shape the mixture into burger patties. Next heat the cooking oil in a large skillet; add the burgers. Brown them on both sides and pour over the Worcestershire sauce and catsup. Reduce the heat to low and cover with lid; let simmer for 1/2 hour.

CHUCKWAGON FRIED COON

1 dressed coon
1 c. cooking oil
1 tsp. vinegar

1 c. cornmeal
1 onion, sliced
Water to cover

Cut the coon into serving portions and parboil for 1 hour or until tender with the onion, water, and vinegar. Roll the coon portions in the cornmeal and fry in a large skillet with the oil until golden brown. Some folks put 1/2 cup flour in with the cornmeal.

LARIAT BARBECUE COON

1 dressed coon
1 tsp. garlic powder
2 c. barbecue sauce
1 tsp. black pepper
3 carrots, chopped

2 celery stalks, chopped
3 onions, chopped
2 bay leaves
3 T. honey
1 tsp. salt

Cut the dressed coon into serving portions and place in a kettle with celery, carrots, onions, bay leaves, salt, pepper, garlic powder, and water to cover. Cook over high heat to boiling until meat is tender (with cover on) about 1 1/2 hours, then drain. Now combine and mix the barbecue sauce and honey together, then place the coon meat in a shallow baking pan and spread the sauce over it. Place the pan in a preheated oven at 350º for 1/2 hour, then serve.

LONESOME DOVE BREASTS AND WINE

10 skinned dove breasts
1 c. chicken bouillon
1 c. white wine
1/8 tsp. black pepper

2 pkgs. dry spaghetti sauce mix
1/2 stick margarine
1/4 tsp. salt

Put spaghetti sauce mix, salt, pepper, and dove in a large bag. Shake well to coat the dove. Next melt margarine in large skillet. Add the coated dove and brown on all sides. Now pour the wine and bouillon into the skillet and cover. Reduce the heat to low and let it simmer about 25 minutes or until breasts are tender. Good over rice.

ANNIE OAKLEY BAKED QUAIL

1/2 tsp. salt
1/4 tsp. pepper

6 quail
6 slices bacon

Salt and pepper quail. Wrap in bacon, then wrap in foil. Place in baking pan in 300° oven for 1 1/2 hours.

WALL DRUG BRAISED QUAIL

4 quail
Salt, pepper, flour
1 can cream of celery soup
1/4 tsp. caraway seed

1/4 c. bacon drippings
1/2 c. milk
1/2 c. chopped onion

Sprinkle quail with salt, pepper, and flour. Brown on all sides in bacon drippings in heavy skillet. Add milk, soup, onion, and caraway. Cover and cook over low heat for 30 minutes or until tender. Baste frequently with pan drippings.

CAJUN FRIED QUAIL

4 quail
1 c. flour
Salt
2 T. cayenne pepper

5 T. Tabasco
1 c. buttermilk
Black pepper
Peanut oil

Mix Tabasco with buttermilk. Split each quail in half. Marinate overnight in buttermilk. Mix flour with salt, pepper, and cayenne. Remove quail from buttermilk and dredge in flour. Half fill skillet with peanut oil. Heat oven to 350°. Add quail. Fry, turning once, until crisp, browned, and tender.

CIMARRON STEWED PRAIRIE CHICKEN

2 prairie chickens
4 slices salt pork

2 onions, quartered
Salt

Soak prairie chickens in salt water for 1 hour. Rinse in clear water. Cut in cubes as for frying. Add onions and salt pork and cover in kettle with boiling water. Cook slowly for 3 hours, letting water almost boil away. Thicken with flour and butter creamed together; salt when half done.

HEELER'S FROG LEGS

Cut off the legs, loosen the outer skin, turn downward, and pull off. Then cut off the skin and the toes. Wash the legs in lightly-salted water. Drain and blanch for 3 minutes in boiling water to which has been added 2 tablespoons vinegar or lemon juice, and a teaspoon of salt for each quart of water. Drain and wipe dry. The frog legs can now be prepared in different ways. If to be fried, dip them in beaten egg and fine cracker or bread crumbs and fry them until nice and brown in enough hot fat to keep from burning.

TURKEY CREEK FRIED FROG

Skin frogs, cut off head, cut into eating pieces. Use all of frog except head, all of it tastes the same. Sprinkle with salt and pepper. Roll in crumbs. Dip in eggs and roll in crumbs again. Fry in very hot fat for about 3 minutes. Drain and serve with melted butter or tartar sauce.

PRAIRIE SHRIMP (Rattlesnake)

After killing a rattlesnake, skin the snake and fillet the meat from the bones. Cut the fillets in about 2-inch long strips. Wash the meat thoroughly. Roll strips in pancake flour and deep fry until golden brown. Seasoning salt may be added to the pancake flour if preferred.

VELVET TAIL RATTLESNAKE

The snakes should be kept alive and in good condition until they are to be eaten. Never bludgeon them with clubs or rocks; the heads should be removed with an axe and disposed of immediately. Then split the body down the belly and remove the skin. You should then gut and clean in fresh water. Due to reflex action, the snake will squirm and wiggle for some time after the head is removed and may crawl out of the pan if left unattended. Dice the snake in about 2-inch pieces using a sharp hatchet or meat cleaver. Soak these pieces overnight in refrigerator in cold salt water. There are 3 good ways to prepare it: (1.) 1 egg, 1 cup milk, and 1 teaspoon salt. Make a batter similar to batter for fried chicken. Roll the pieces in this batter and then in equal parts of cracker crumbs and flour. Deep fat fry until golden brown. (2.) Fix as above but instead of deep frying, pan fry and then simmer in 1 cup of water until tender as you would Southern fried chicken. (3.) Baste meat with barbecue sauce and cook on grill. This is somewhat drier but many prefer this method.

SCARED PRAIRIE CHICKEN

Dress and plunge into cold water. Drain, but do not wipe. Sprinkle with salt and pepper and coat thickly with flour, allowing as much flour as possible to adhere to the bird. Cook slowly in hot fat, which is part butter, until tender and brown. Garnish with parsley and accompany with a milk gravy after removing chicken from the pan.

NORTH PLATTE ROAST WILD TURKEY IN A SACK

Grease a brown paper bag inside with melted shortening. Brush turkey with melted shortening, salt and pepper. Make a dressing, adding oysters or mushrooms, and stuff bird. Fit turkey into the greased bag, twist end, and tie with string. Place in pan and bake in moderate oven (325°) for 24 minutes per pound. When done, remove from oven, but do not open sack for at least 20 minutes. This allows the turkey to absorb the steam for moister meat.

FORT ROBINSON WILD TURKEY CHOP SUEY

1 c. chopped celery	1 c. chopped onion
2 pork chops	Leftover turkey
Water	Soy sauce
1 (#2) can bean sprouts	1 (4-oz.) can mushrooms
2 T. cornstarch	1 (#2¹/₂) can Chinese noodles

Simmer leftover turkey in water in a large covered saucepan until meat falls off the bone. Remove bones and drain meat, reserving broth. Saute celery and onion until soft, but not browned. Fry pork chops and cut into bite-sized pieces. To broth, add enough soy sauce for a deep brown color. Add cornstarch diluted with water and cook until thickened. Add turkey, pork, onion, celery, bean sprouts, and mushrooms. Heat and serve over crisp Chinese noodles.

SAND HILLS SMOTHERED GROUSE

4 grouse	1/4 c. chopped celery
1 T. salt	1/4 c. chopped carrot
1/2 c. flour	1/4 c. chopped onion
1/2 c. boiling water	4 T. butter

Skin, wash, and quarter grouse. Mix flour and salt in paper bag. Shake grouse pieces with flour until coated. Melt 2 tablespoons butter in skillet. Saute celery, carrot, and onion until tender. Place in shallow baking pan. Add 2 more tablespoons butter to skillet and melt. Brown floured grouse. Remove meat to baking pan. Add water, and cover. Bake in preheated oven at 350° for 1 hour.

WAGON TONGUE GROUSE IN SOUR CREAM

Cut 2 plump grouse into serving pieces, and dredge in flour. Melt 1/4 cup butter in a large skillet, and saute grouse over moderate heat until golden on all sides. Sprinkle with salt and pepper. Lower heat and continue to cook until grouse is tender. Remove to serving platter and keep hot. To the juices in the pan, add 2 tablespoons flour and gradually stir in 2 cups warm, but not boiled, sour cream. Cook, stirring to blend, all the rich brown bits with the cream, until the sauce is very hot and slightly thickened. Pour sauce over grouse. Serve with wild rice and mushrooms.

CRIPPLE CREEK ROAST WILD GOOSE

1 young wild goose, 6-8 lbs. dressed	Juice of 1 lemon
	Seasonings
6 slices bacon	Melted lard or shortening
1 tart apple	1 med. onion

Rub goose inside and out with lemon juice, salt, and pepper. Place apple and onion inside and truss. Cover breast with bacon and a square of foil. Place in heavy roaster on rack or cumbled foil. Roast in slow oven (300⁰) for about 2 hours or more until tender. Baste with pan drippings or additional shortening. Add 1 cup boiling water to roaster if meat seems dry. Discard apple and onion when cooking is completed. An onion dressing or Stove Top dressing balls are good, too. **Note:** Grouse can be roasted in the same way. Currant jelly with a dash of horseradish makes a tasty accompaniment.

PLATTE RIVER WILD GOOSE

Soak goose for several hours in salt water. Put a small onion inside and plunge it into boiling water 20 minutes. Stuff with chopped celery, chopped eggs, mashed potatoes, bits of fat pork or other cold meat, a little butter, raw grated turnip, a tablespoon of pepper vinegar, a little chopped onion, salt to taste. A cup of stock or broth must be placed in the pan with the fowl. Butter the goose and dredge with flour. Baste often. Pin a buttered paper over the breast to prevent it becoming hard. Serve with mushroom or celery sauce, or for a simpler taste, with its own gravy.

TRAILSIDE FRIED RABBIT

2 rabbits, cut into serving
  chunks
Salt

1 c. flour
Pepper

Put rabbit in boiling water. Simmer for 20 minutes. Drain. Dry mix flour, salt, and pepper. Roll rabbit in flour; fry in hot lard. If you would like gravy, drain most of lard off after all frying is done. Save about 3 tablespoons. Pour in 1 cup of buttermilk and simmer - **do not boil** - scraping the bottom of the frying pan.

SPORTSMAN'S RABBIT DELIGHT

1 rabbit, cut-up
1 tsp. pepper
2 bay leaves
1/2 c. molasses
Equal parts of vinegar and
  water

1 tsp. salt
1 lg. onion
1 stalk celery
2 apples, sliced
Flour, butter, or oil

Place rabbit in marinade made by combining next 8 ingredients. Let stand overnight. Cook for 2 hours. Remove rabbit from liquid. Sprinkle with flour. Brown in butter, turning from side to side. Add about 2 cups of the marinade. Simmer until tender. Brown flour; add to remaining liquid until all at desired consistency. Pour over rabbit on platter. Yields 4-6 servings.

TEXAS FRIED SQUIRREL

2 dressed squirrels
1 (5-oz.) jar sliced mushrooms
1/2 stick margarine
4 T. water
1 c. sour cream

1 c. flour
1/2 tsp. salt
1/2 tsp. black pepper
1/2 c. sherry

Cut the dressed squirrels into serving portions and sprinkle with salt and pepper; then roll in the flour. Melt the margarine in a skillet over medium heat. Add the squirrel to the skillet; slowly fry and brown on all sides. Remove the done squirrel to a warm platter and make the gravy by adding 2 tablespoons flour and 2 table-spoons water to the skillet, stirring until smooth and thickened. Now add the sour cream, sherry, and drained mushrooms to the skillet. Stir until smooth, then pour the hot gravy over the golden brown squirrel and serve.

ROCKY'S SQUIRREL CASSEROLE

Place one or two young squirrels, clean and cut in pieces, in large pan and add salt and enough water to cover well. Bring to a hard boil. Pour liquid off; rinse in cold water. In casserole or flat pan that has been buttered, slice potatoes. Season with salt and pepper to taste. Place squirrel on top. Put enough milk and pats of butter to cover potatoes well. Season with garlic, onion bits, thyme, oregano, and caraway seeds to taste. Cook at 325° for 1 hour or until meat is tender. Remove lid to brown.

ROAST BEAVER

10-lb. beaver	3 lbs. onions, sliced
1 pt. plum jelly	1/2 c. salt
1 tsp. pepper	

Remove all fat from beaver. Cut into 1 1/2-pound pieces. Wash and pack in alternate layers with onions in a large granite or plastic pan. Cover with ice cubes; let stand overnight. Drain and wash several times. Place beaver in layers with plum jelly, salt, and pepper in roaster. Bake at 375° for about 3 hours.

BIG TIMBER BARBECUED BEAVER

3 T. bacon drippings	2 tsp. chili powder
2 T. water	1/4 c. vinegar
1/2 c. catsup	1 lg. onion, chopped fine
3 tsp. salt	1 tsp. paprika
1/8 tsp. garlic powder	

Roast beaver until meat comes off bones and shred it into small pieces. Mix the above barbecue sauce as to the amount you need for your meat (this should cover about 2 1/2 pounds of meat). Let your meat simmer in this for a short time. Serve hot on buns.

WAGON TRAIN WILD DUCK

4 wild wood ducks	4 T. butter, softened
4 apples	Salt & ground pepper
3 lg. onions	3/4 c. brandy
4 celery ribs with tops	3/4 c. currant jelly

Clean and dry ducks, inside and out. Stuff each duck with a piece or two of apple, onion, and celery. Brush all with softened butter. Rub the duck well with butter and season with salt and pepper. Melt the currant jelly. Combine with brandy and baste duck. Place ducks in large roasting pan on a rack and roast at 400°, basting with currant jelly mixture every 10 minutes. Cook 35-40 minutes for rare, 45-50 minutes for medium. Transfer to serving plate and pour over the pan juices.

MOCK WILD RICE AND DUCK

1 1/3 c. instant rice
1 1/2 c. finely-chopped
  mushrooms
1/4 c. finely-chopped onions
1 1/2 tsp. salt
Dash of pepper
1 1/3 c. broth

1/4 c. butter
1 c. finely-chopped celery
1/4 c. finely-chopped celery
  leaves
1/4 tsp. marjoram
Pinch of sage or thyme
1/3 c. chopped pecans

Cook a mallard duck in the same manner you would a chicken. Remove all meat from the bone and reserve the broth. Put all ingredients except pecans in a pan with a lid. Mix lightly and bring to a boil. Simmer for 2 minutes, then allow to set for 10 minutes with lid on. Remove lid and fluff rice mixture with a fork. Add the duck meat and pecans. Keep hot and serve at once. (This works great for those ducks that were badly shot up and had to be skinned.)

INDIAN PAINT BRUSH PHEASANT IN SOUR CREAM

2 pheasants, cut in serving
  pieces
2 tsp. salt
1 can mushroom soup
1 tsp. pepper
1/2 c. flour
1 c. sour cream

1 c. salad oil
1 pkg. dry onion soup
Milk
Salt
Pepper
Flour
Cooking oil

Sprinkle pheasant with salt and pepper. Dredge in flour. Fry in oil until brown. Place in casserole and pour off excess oil. Make gravy from cream soup, sour cream, dry soup, and milk. Pour gravy over pheasant and bake at 325° for 1 hour.

WAGON SPOKE FRENCH-FRIED PHEASANT

2 pheasants
1 c. flour, salt, & pepper

1 beaten egg
Cooking oil

Remove skin and bones from whole pheasant. Cube meat and dip in beaten egg, then flour. Fry in hot oil until lightly browned. Serve hot. If preferred, make ahead of time and refrigerate. When ready to use, reheat in 350° oven for 10 minutes.

BROKEN BOW ROAST PHEASANT

1 pheasant
2 T. chopped onion
1/2 tsp. sage or more to taste
1/4 c. melted oleo
Bacon slices

5 slices bread, torn in pieces
1/8 tsp. salt
Dash of pepper
1 egg, beaten
1/4 c. chopped celery

Wash and dry skinned bird. Mix bread, celery, onion, salt, pepper, sage, oleo, and egg. Add a little hot water for a moister dressing. Stuff bird loosely with mixture and place on rack in Dutch oven. Cover bird with bacon strips. Cover pan and roast for 1-1 1/4 hours at 350°.

TURKEY CREEK BOILED CRAYFISH

To clean: Put in a tub; cover with screen and run clear water through them until they clean themselves. Plunge them into a large kettle of boiling water so they die quickly. Add salt and boil until the crayfish are bright pink. These are good peeled and dipped in butter, or the tails can be peeled. Be sure to remove the vein and discard and serve as cold shrimp cocktail.

TIMBERLINE MOOSE POT ROAST

Select a 5 or 6-pound chunk portion. Place in a large stainless steel bowl or an earthenware crock. Mix with a quart of water: 2 medium-sized sliced onions, a stalk of diced celery, 1 tablespoon sugar, 1 teaspoon salt, and 1/2 teaspoon each of curry powder, thyme, rosemary, mace, and freshly-ground black pepper. Pour over the moose meat and marinate for a day and a night. Sear the meat with a tablespoon of butter or margarine in a very hot (450°) oven for 15 minutes. Then pour the marinade back over it. Cover and bake in a moderate (325°) oven for a couple of hours or until tender. Fork the meat onto a hot platter. Blend 2 tablespoons of soft butter or margarine with 2 tablespoons of flour and stir smoothly into the gravy. Cook until thick.

YELLOWSTONE CARIBOU STEAK IN CASSEROLE

Cut 4 pounds of boneless steak 1 inch thick from the tougher portion of a caribou quarter and separate into 1-pound servings. Place in a glass, crockery, earthenware, or stainless steel container. Add a cup of dry Burgundy, 3 tablespoons vegetable oil, a minced clove of garlic, and 1/2 teaspoon dried rosemary. Marinate 1 1/2 hours, then saving the liquid, remove the steaks and wipe each dry with paper toweling. Starting with a cold fry pan, cook 8 slices of bacon over moderate heat until they are golden brown. Then remove the bacon. Break it up and put to one side. Brown the meat on both sides in the remaining grease. Then lay the steaks in a large casserole. Add the bits of bacon and a 1 1/2 pound package of frozen stew vegetables. Pour off all but about 2 tablespoons of the bacon fat and juices from the fry pan. Sprinkle what remains with flour and mix well. Slowly and smoothly stir in the marinade, along with a double-strength cup of beef bouillon or the equivalent. Bring to a simmer. Turn this over the caribou and vegetables in the casserole and warm everything to a bubble. Cover and bake in a moderate 350° oven for about 2 hours or until the steaks are tender.

BIG HORN ELK GOULASH

Dice 3 pounds of the toughest part of the animal. Dredge in 2 tablespoons flour, 3 teaspoons paprika, 1 teaspoon salt, and 1/4 teaspoon freshly-ground black pepper. Then brown along with 3 cups diced onions in 1/2 stick of butter or margarine and 1 tablespoon of cooking oil. Add 2 cups diced potatoes and a slice of garlic. Pour in a cup of beef bouillon. Cover tightly and simmer until the elk is tender, adding a bit of water if necessary. Adjust the salt and serve.

BLACK HILLS BUFFALO RIB ROAST

Bone, roll, and tie a 4-pound chuck of this tender meat. Roll in flour. In a Dutch oven atop the stove, brown the section of buffalo thoroughly in 1/2 stick of melted butter and margarine. Add a cup of diced onion, 1/2 cup diced carrot, the contents of a small can of sliced mushrooms, and a minced clove of garlic. Saute until these, too, are brown. Pour in 2 cups dry Burgundy, 1/2 teaspoon lemon pepper, 1/4 teaspoon thyme, 1/4 teaspoon marjoram, and salt to taste. Cover and bake some 3 hours in a moderate 325° oven or until the meat is fork tender, adding more wine if necessary. Shift the roast to a hot platter. Strain the liquid, adjust its seasoning, and pour over the buffalo.

BOOT LEGGER BUFFALO ALA MODE

Place a 4-5 pound chunk of round or rump, larded unless there is already some fat on it in a deep stainless steel, pottery, or glass bowl with 2 cups Burgundy, 1 tablespoon salt, 1 teaspoon each of thyme, marjoram, and cloves, and 1/2 teaspoon freshly-ground black pepper, 4 medium-sized sliced onions, 3 medium-sized sliced carrots, and a small sliced stalk of celery with the leaves. Prepare one afternoon and let it stand, covered, until the next. Then fork out the meat and dry it with paper towels. Strain the liquid. Warm a Dutch oven over high heat, swiping it liberally with bison or beef fat. Then brown the meat thoroughly. Keep it off the bottom afterwards with a rack or such so that it will not stick; pour on the strained liquid. Cover. Lower the heat and simmer very slowly for 3 hours or until a testing fork proves it to be tender. Have at least an inch of liquid in the bottom throughout, adding more Burgundy if this should become necessary. Once the buffalo is tender, remove it and the fluid separately from the pot. Skim the fat off the juices. Taste and if necessary, adjust the salt. Then return the meat and the juices to the Dutch oven and basting, cook very slowly another 15 minutes. Have enough sliced carrots and tiny onions for dinner all cooked. Add these, hot, to the Dutch oven the last 5 minutes. Serve, steaming with the dark gravy.

LONGBRANCH CARIBOU LIVER

Slice about 1½-pound portion of caribou liver very thin. Then, using a sharp knife and a carving board, cut the liver across into very thin, matchlike pieces. Saute half a dozen, medium-sized, thinly-sliced onions in 1/2 stick of margarine or butter in the fry pan until the onion soften. Then, stirring, saute the liver for 2 minutes, only until it loses its redness. Season to taste with salt, freshly-gound black pepper, and parsley flakes. Serve with hot baking powder biscuits.

STAGECOACH CARIBOU TONGUE

Caribou tongue is a delicacy. Cut out by making a slit under the lower jaw, drawing the tongue down through this, and severing it at the root. Scrub it well, but, as with all game meat, do not soak. Instead cover with boiling water. Add a sliced onion, a quartered clove of garlic, 1 tablespoon salt, ¼ teaspoon freshly-ground black pepper, 6 whole cloves, and a bay leaf. Simmer about 1 hour per pound or until a sharp fork can be easily inserted and withdrawn. Then fork out the tongue. Immerse in cold water. Slit the skin and peel it off, and cut the bones and gristle at the thick end. The tongue can then be reheated in its own juice before serving, thinly sliced, or it can be relished cold. Or for something special, saute a pound of fresh sliced mushrooms in 3 tablespoons butter or margarine. Add 2 cans of concentrated mushroom soup and ½ can water. Bring to simmer. Season with ½ teaspoon nutmeg, ¼ teaspoon cinnamon, and ⅛ teaspoon cloves. Add a jigger of Metaxa brandy. Slice enough tongue for four. Place with the sauce in a shallow casserole and warm everything.

FORT BENT ANTELOPE CUTLETS IN SOUR CREAM

Cut your slices ½ inch thick from an antelope hind quarter. For some 2 pounds of these, enough to serve 4, melt a stick of butter or margarine in a heavy fry pan. Rub proportionately 1 teaspoon salt and ⅛ teaspoon freshly-ground black pepper into the cutlets, then dust well with flour. Brown on both sides over low heat. Then pour 2 cups of sour cream over the meat. Simmer until just tender. Shake on paprika and parsley flakes for added taste.

GENERIC BAKED BOAR CHOPS

Season 4 loin chops. Cut about 2 inches thick, to taste, with salt and freshly-ground black pepper, then dredge in flour. Melt ½ stick butter or margarine in a heavy fry pan and brown the chops on both sides. Then remove the meat to a baking pan. Stir ½ cup sour cream, ½ cup water, 2 tablespoons vinegar, 2 teaspoons sugar, and 2 teaspoons summer savory into the drippings in the fry pan. Bring to a bubble and cascade over the chops. Cover and bake in a moderate 325° oven 1¾ hours.

RED LODGE BEAR KIDNEYS

Strip away connective tissues from kidneys; then cut and divide them into segments the size of chicken hearts. Simmer in butter with salt, cloves, celery, and onion until tender. Serve over mashed potatoes.

ROUGH RIDERS BAKED BEAR CHOPS

Trim all but about 1/4 inch of any fat from the chops which for this recipe should be about 1 1/2 inches thick. Set in a deep baking pan. Strew with salt and freshly-ground black pepper to taste. Spread a teaspoon of brown sugar atop each chop and place a slice of lemon atop each. Mix a cup of tomato catsup and a cup of water, more of both if necessary, and barely cover the chops with the fluid. Bake in a moderate 325° oven 1 1/2 hours or until well done and tender.

Robert E. Kerby

WAGON SPOKE ROAST BEAR

Bear meat must be well done. Marinating will disguise the true flavor, so it is not recommended. Do not season, flour, or sear. Set the meat on a rack in an open pan with the bone, if any, toward the bottom. Use a moderate oven, 325°, and roast until a large sharp fork can be easily inserted and withdrawn. Baste frequently after the first hour.

DEER TRAIL MARINATED MOUNTAIN GOAT RIBS

Saw 4 pounds of short ribs into serving portions. Spread flat over the bottom of a large pan. In a separate pot, mix 2 cups chopped onions, 8-ounce can of tomato sauce, 1 cup concentrated beef bouillon, 1 tablespoon Worcestershire sauce, 1 tablespoon prepared horseradish, 2 teaspoons sugar, 1 teaspoon each of wine vinegar, salt, and dry mustard, and 1/8 teaspoon freshly-ground black pepper. Bring to a bubble for 10 minutes. Pour hot over the meat. Marinate for 8 hours, turning several times. Then shift the ribs and the marinade to a Dutch oven. Cover and simmer for 3 hours or until tender, spooning the marinade over the meat occasionally.

Robert E. Kerby
8/K 1982

LONGHORN PORCUPINE MULLIGAN

Trim off excess fat from a 4-5 pound chunk of porcupine. Cut into pieces and brown in butter or margarine using a heavy cast iron pot or Dutch oven. Add 2 cups water, 1 cup Burgundy, the juice of a lemon, a diced clove of garlic, 2 bay leaves, 2 teaspoons salt, ¼ teaspoon freshly-ground black pepper, and ⅛ teaspoon each of powdered cloves, ground nutmeg, allspice, and paprika. Keep covered and cook slowly for 1½ hours or until the meat is nearly tender. Add more salt if necessary and remove the bay leaves. Stir in medium sized chunks of potatoes, onions, and celery. Cover and continue cooking slowly another 20 minutes or until vegetables are done.

PIKES PEAK MOOSE NOSE

One of the great gourmet delights of the North American wilderness is prepared from such an unlikely object as a moose nose. To get at this, cut off the large upper jaw just below the eyes. Simmer in a pot of bubbling water for an hour. Cool and pull out the loosened hairs. Wash clean. Then return to the scoured pot. Add fresh water, salt, and freshly-ground black pepper to taste, and 3 quartered onions. Cook just short of boiling until the dark meat falls away from the bones and jowls and white strips ease from the nostrils. Alternate bits of both kinds of meat in a small narrow pan; strain the liquid over them. Let the juices and the meat jell together overnight, and savor the whole in cold slices.

PROSPECTOR'S MOOSE STEW

Start by cutting 3 pounds of moose quarter or pot roast into bite-sized squares. Brown these, along with 6 cups of sliced onions, with a stick of butter or margarine in the bottom of a heavy Dutch oven. Add a cup of sliced mushrooms, a can of concentrated beef bouillon, a sugar bottle of beer, 2 sliced cloves of garlic, 2 tablespoons brown sugar, 2 tablespoons chopped parsley, ½ teaspoon thyme, and a bay leaf. Cover and simmer for 1½-3 hours or until the moose is tender. Then thicken with 2 tablespoons of cornstarch and 2 tablespoons vinegar.

ELEPHANT STEW

1 elephant   **2 rabbits, opt.**
Salt & pepper

Oven Temperature: 450⁰. Baking Time: 4 weeks. Cut elephant into bite-sized pieces. This should take about 2 months. Add enough brown gravy to cover. Cook over kerosene stove about 4 weeks at 450⁰. This will feed 3800 cowhands. If more are expected, 2 rabbits may be added, but do only if necessary, because most people do not like hares in their stew.

Robert Kirby

INDEX OF RECIPES

MAIN DISHES AND CASSEROLES

MEAT, POULTRY, AND SEAFOOD

BREADS AND ROLLS

PIES, PASTRY, AND DESSERTS

CAKES, COOKIES, AND CANDY

PANTRY BASICS

A WELL-STOCKED PANTRY provides all the makings for a good meal. With the right ingredients, you can quickly create a variety of satisfying, delicious meals for family or guests. Keeping these items in stock also means avoiding extra trips to the grocery store, saving you time and money. Although everyone's pantry is different, there are basic items you should always have. Add other items according to your family's needs. For example, while some families consider chips, cereals and snacks as must-haves, others can't be without feta cheese and imported olives. Use these basic pantry suggestions as a handy reference list when creating your grocery list. Don't forget refrigerated items like milk, eggs, cheese and butter.

STAPLES

Baker's chocolate
Baking powder
Baking soda
Barbeque sauce
Bread crumbs (plain or seasoned)
Chocolate chips
Cocoa powder
Cornmeal
Cornstarch
Crackers
Flour
Honey
Ketchup
Lemon juice
Mayonnaise or salad dressing
Non-stick cooking spray
Nuts (almonds, pecans, walnuts)
Oatmeal
Oil (olive, vegetable)
Pancake baking mix
Pancake syrup
Peanut butter
Shortening
Sugar (granulated, brown, powdered)
Vinegar

PACKAGED/CANNED FOODS

Beans (canned, dry)
Broth (beef, chicken)
Cake mixes with frosting
Canned diced tomatoes
Canned fruit
Canned mushrooms
Canned soup
Canned tomato paste & sauce
Canned tuna & chicken
Cereal
Dried soup mix
Gelatin (flavored or plain)
Gravies
Jarred Salsa
Milk (evaporated, sweetened condensed)
Non-fat dry milk
Pastas
Rice (brown, white)
Spaghetti sauce

SPICES/SEASONINGS

Basil
Bay leaves
Black pepper
Boullion cubes (beef, chicken)
Chives
Chili powder
Cinnamon
Mustard (dried, prepared)
Garlic powder or salt
Ginger
Nutmeg
Onion powder or salt
Oregano
Paprika
Parsley
Rosemary
Sage
Salt
Soy sauce
Tarragon
Thyme
Vanilla
Worcestershire sauce
Yeast

FLOUR

HERBS & SPICES

DRIED VS. FRESH. While dried herbs are convenient, they don't generally have the same purity of flavor as fresh herbs. Ensure dried herbs are still fresh by checking if they are green and not faded. Crush a few leaves to see if the aroma is still strong. Always store them in an air-tight container away from light and heat.

BASIL — Sweet, warm flavor with an aromatic odor. Use whole or ground. Good with lamb, fish, roast, stews, beef, vegetables, dressing and omelets.

BAY LEAVES — Pungent flavor. Use whole leaf but remove before serving. Good in vegetable dishes, seafood, stews and pickles.

CARAWAY — Spicy taste and aromatic smell. Use in cakes, breads, soups, cheese and sauerkraut.

CELERY SEED — Strong taste which resembles the vegetable. Can be used sparingly in pickles and chutney, meat and fish dishes, salads, bread, marinades, dressings and dips.

CHIVES — Sweet, mild flavor like that of onion. Excellent in salads, fish, soups and potatoes.

CILANTRO — Use fresh. Excellent in salads, fish, chicken, rice, beans and Mexican dishes.

CINNAMON — Sweet, pungent flavor. Widely used in many sweet baked goods, chocolate dishes, cheesecakes, pickles, chutneys and hot drinks.

CORIANDER — Mild, sweet, orangy flavor and available whole or ground. Common in curry powders and pickling spice and also used in chutney, meat dishes, casseroles, Greek-style dishes, apple pies and baked goods.

CURRY POWDER — Spices are combined to proper proportions to give a distinct flavor to meat, poultry, fish and vegetables.

DILL — Both seeds and leaves are flavorful. Leaves may be used as a garnish or cooked with fish, soup, dressings, potatoes and beans. Leaves or the whole plant may be used to flavor pickles.

FENNEL — Sweet, hot flavor. Both seeds and leaves are used. Use in small quantities in pies and baked goods. Leaves can be boiled with fish.

DILL
Seeds

HERBS & SPICES

GINGER
A pungent root, this aromatic spice is sold fresh, dried or ground. Use in pickles, preserves, cakes, cookies, soups and meat dishes.

MARJORAM
May be used both dried or green. Use to flavor fish, poultry, omelets, lamb, stew, stuffing and tomato juice.

MINT
Aromatic with a cool flavor. Excellent in beverages, fish, lamb, cheese, soup, peas, carrots and fruit desserts.

NUTMEG
Whole or ground. Used in chicken and cream soups, cheese dishes, fish cakes, and with chicken and veal. Excellent in custards, milk puddings, pies and cakes.

OREGANO
Strong, aromatic odor. Use whole or ground in tomato juice, fish, eggs, pizza, omelets, chili, stew, gravy, poultry and vegetables.

PAPRIKA
A bright red pepper, this spice is used in meat, vegetables and soups or as a garnish for potatoes, salads or eggs.

PARSLEY
Best when used fresh, but can be used dried as a garnish or as a seasoning. Try in fish, omelets, soup, meat, stuffing and mixed greens.

ROSEMARY
Very aromatic. Can be used fresh or dried. Season fish, stuffing, beef, lamb, poultry, onions, eggs, bread and potatoes. Great in dressings.

SAFFRON
Aromatic, slightly bitter taste. Only a pinch needed to flavor and color dishes such as bouillabaisse, chicken soup, rice, paella, fish sauces, buns and cakes. Very expensive, so where a touch of color is needed, use turmeric instead, but the flavor will not be the same.

SAGE
Use fresh or dried. The flowers are sometimes used in salads. May be used in tomato juice, fish, omelets, beef, poultry, stuffing, cheese spreads and breads.

TARRAGON
Leaves have a pungent, hot taste. Use to flavor sauces, salads, fish, poultry, tomatoes, eggs, green beans, carrots and dressings.

THYME
Sprinkle leaves on fish or poultry before broiling or baking. Throw a few sprigs directly on coals shortly before meat is finished grilling.

TURMERIC
Aromatic, slightly bitter flavor. Should be used sparingly in curry powder and relishes and to color cakes and rice dishes.

Use 3 times more fresh herbs if substituting fresh for dried.

BAKING BREADS

HINTS FOR BAKING BREADS

- Kneading dough for 30 seconds after mixing improves the texture of baking powder biscuits.

- Instead of shortening, use cooking or salad oil in waffles and hot cakes.

- When bread is baking, a small dish of water in the oven will help keep the crust from hardening.

- Dip a spoon in hot water to measure shortening, butter, etc., and the fat will slip out more easily.

- Small amounts of leftover corn may be added to pancake batter for variety.

- To make bread crumbs, use the fine cutter of a food grinder and tie a large paper bag over the spout in order to prevent flying crumbs.

- When you are doing any sort of baking, you get better results if you remember to preheat your cookie sheet, muffin tins or cake pans.

3 RULES FOR USE OF LEAVENING AGENTS

1. In simple flour mixtures, use 2 teaspoons baking powder to leaven 1 cup flour. Reduce this amount 1/2 teaspoon for each egg used.

2. To 1 teaspoon soda, use 2 1/4 teaspoons cream of tartar, 2 cups freshly soured milk or 1 cup molasses.

3. To substitute soda and an acid for baking powder, divide the amount of baking powder by 4. Take that as your measure and add acid according to rule 2.

PROPORTIONS OF BAKING POWDER TO FLOUR

biscuits ....to 1 cup flour use 1 1/4 tsp. baking powder
cake with oil ....to 1 cup flour use 1 tsp. baking powder
muffins ....to 1 cup flour use 1 1/2 tsp. baking powder
popovers ....to 1 cup flour use 1 1/4 tsp. baking powder
waffles ....to 1 cup flour use 1 1/4 tsp. baking powder

PROPORTIONS OF LIQUID TO FLOUR

pour batter ....to 1 cup liquid use 1 cup flour
drop batter ....to 1 cup liquid use 2 to 2 1/2 cups flour
soft dough ....to 1 cup liquid use 3 to 3 1/2 cups flour
stiff dough ....to 1 cup liquid use 4 cups flour

TIME & TEMPERATURE CHART

Breads	Minutes	Temperature
biscuits	12 - 15	400° - 450°
cornbread	25 - 30	400° - 425°
gingerbread	40 - 50	350° - 370°
loaf	50 - 60	350° - 400°
nut bread	50 - 75	350°
popovers	30 - 40	425° - 450°
rolls	20 - 30	400° - 450°

BAKING DESSERTS

PERFECT COOKIES

Cookie dough that must be rolled is much easier to handle after it has been refrigerated for 10 to 30 minutes. This keeps the dough from sticking, even though it may be soft. If not done, the soft dough may require more flour and too much flour makes cookies hard and brittle. Place on a floured board only as much dough as can be easily managed. Flour the rolling pin slightly and roll lightly to desired thickness. Cut shapes close together and add trimmings to dough that needs to be rolled. Place pans or sheets in upper third of oven. Watch cookies carefully while baking in order to avoid burned edges. When sprinkling sugar on cookies, try putting it into a salt shaker in order to save time.

PERFECT PIES

• Pie crust will be better and easier to make if all the ingredients are cool.

• The lower crust should be placed in the pan so that it covers the surface smoothly. Air pockets beneath the surface will push the crust out of shape while baking.

• Folding the top crust over the lower crust before crimping will keep juices in the pie.

• When making custard pie, bake at a high temperature for about 10 minutes to prevent a soggy crust. Then finish baking at a low temperature.

• When making cream pie, sprinkle crust with powdered sugar in order to prevent it from becoming soggy.

PERFECT CAKES

• Fill cake pans two-thirds full and spread batter into corners and sides, leaving a slight hollow in the center.

• Cake is done when it shrinks from the sides of the pan or if it springs back when touched lightly with the finger.

• After removing a cake from the oven, place it on a rack for about 5 minutes. Then, the sides should be loosened and the cake turned out on a rack in order to finish cooling.

• Do not frost cakes until thoroughly cool.

• Icing will remain where you put it if you sprinkle cake with powdered sugar first.

TIME & TEMPERATURE CHART

Dessert	Time	Temperature
butter cake, layer	20-40 min.	380° - 400°
butter cake, loaf	40-60 min.	360° - 400°
cake, angel	50-60 min.	300° - 360°
cake, fruit	3-4 hrs.	275° - 325°
cake, sponge	40-60 min.	300° - 350°
cookies, molasses	18-20 min.	350° - 375°
cookies, thin	10-12 min.	380° - 390°
cream puffs	45-60 min.	300° - 350°
meringue	40-60 min.	250° - 300°
pie crust	20-40 min.	400° - 500°

VEGETABLES & FRUITS

COOKING TIME TABLE

Vegetable	Cooking Method	Time
artichokes	boiled	40 min.
	steamed	45-60 min.
asparagus tips	boiled	10-15 min.
beans, lima	boiled	20-40 min.
	steamed	60 min.
beans, string	boiled	15-35 min.
	steamed	60 min.
beets, old	boiled or steamed	1-2 hours.
beets, young with skin	boiled	30 min.
	steamed	60 min.
	baked	70-90 min.
broccoli, flowerets	boiled	5-10 min.
broccoli, stems	boiled	20-30 min.
brussels sprouts	boiled	20-30 min.
cabbage, chopped	boiled	10-20 min.
	steamed	25 min.
carrots, cut across	boiled	8-10 min.
	steamed	40 min.
cauliflower, flowerets	boiled	8-10 min.
cauliflower, stem down	boiled	20-30 min.
corn, green, tender	boiled	5-10 min.
	steamed	15 min.
	baked	20 min.
corn on the cob	boiled	8-10 min.
	steamed	15 min.
eggplant, whole	boiled	30 min.
	steamed	40 min.
	baked	45 min.
parsnips	boiled	25-40 min.
	steamed	60 min.
	baked	60-75 min.
peas, green	boiled or steamed	5-15 min.
potatoes	boiled	20-40 min.
	steamed	60 min.
	baked	45-60 min.
pumpkin or squash	boiled	20-40 min.
	steamed	45 min.
	baked	60 min.
tomatoes	boiled	5-15 min.
turnips	boiled	25-40 min.

DRYING TIME TABLE

Fruit	Sugar or Honey	Cooking Time
apricots	1/4 c. for each cup of fruit	about 40 min.
figs	1 T. for each cup of fruit	about 30 min.
peaches	1/4 c. for each cup of fruit	about 45 min.
prunes	2 T. for each cup of fruit	about 45 min.

VEGETABLES & FRUITS

BUYING FRESH VEGETABLES

Artichokes: Look for compact, tightly closed heads with green, clean-looking leaves. Avoid those with leaves that are brown or separated.

Asparagus: Stalks should be tender and firm; tips should be close and compact. Choose the stalks with very little white; they are more tender. Use asparagus soon because it toughens quickly.

Beans, Snap: Those with small seeds inside the pods are best. Avoid beans with dry-looking pods.

Broccoli, Brussels Sprouts and Cauliflower: Flower clusters on broccoli and cauliflower should be tight and close together. Brussels sprouts should be firm and compact. Smudgy, dirty spots may indicate pests or disease.

Cabbage and Head Lettuce: Choose heads that are heavy for their size. Avoid cabbage with worm holes and lettuce with discoloration or soft rot.

Cucumbers: Choose long, slender cucumbers for best quality. May be dark or medium green, but yellow ones are undesirable.

Mushrooms: Caps should be closed around the stems. Avoid black or brown gills.

Peas and Lima Beans: Select pods that are well-filled but not bulging. Avoid dried, spotted, yellow or limp pods.

BUYING FRESH FRUITS

Bananas: Skin should be free of bruises and black or brown spots. Purchase them slightly green and allow them to ripen at room temperature.

Berries: Select plump, solid berries with good color. Avoid stained containers which indicate wet or leaky berries. Berries with clinging caps, such as blackberries and raspberries, may be unripe. Strawberries without caps may be overripe.

Melons: In cantaloupes, thick, close netting on the rind indicates best quality. Canta-loupes are ripe when the stem scar is smooth and the space between the netting is yellow or yellow-green. They are best when fully ripe with fruity odor.

Honeydews are ripe when rind has creamy to yellowish color and velvety texture. Immature honeydews are whitish-green.

Ripe watermelons have some yellow color on one side. If melons are white or pale green on one side, they are not ripe.

Oranges, Grapefruit and Lemons: Choose those heavy for their size. Smoother, thinner skins usually indicate more juice. Most skin markings do not affect quality. Oranges with a slight greenish tinge may be just as ripe as fully colored ones. Light or greenish-yellow lemons are more tart than deep yellow ones. Avoid citrus fruits showing withered, sunken or soft areas.

NAPKIN FOLDING

FOR BEST RESULTS, use well-starched linen napkins if possible. For more complicated folds, 24-inch napkins work best. Practice the folds with newspapers. Children will have fun decorating the table once they learn these attractive folds!

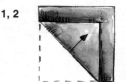

1, 2

3

4

SHIELD

Easy fold. Elegant with monogram in corner.

Instructions:
1. Fold into quarter size. If monogrammed, ornate corner should face down.
2. Turn up folded corner three-quarters.
3. Overlap right side and left side points.
4. Turn over; adjust sides so they are even, single point in center.
5. Place point up or down on plate, or left of plate.

ROSETTE

Elegant on plate.

Instructions:
1. Fold left and right edges to center, leaving ½" opening along center.
2. Pleat firmly from top edge to bottom edge. Sharpen edges with hot iron.
3. Pinch center together. If necessary, use small piece of pipe cleaner to secure and top with single flower.
4. Spread out rosette.

1

2

3

4

NAPKIN FOLDING

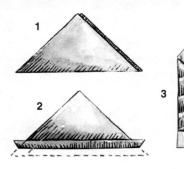

CANDLE

Easy to do; can be decorated.

Instructions:
1. Fold into triangle, point at top.
2. Turn lower edge up 1".
3. Turn over, folded edge down.
4. Roll tightly from left to right.
5. Tuck in corner. Stand upright.

FAN

Pretty in napkin ring or on plate.

Instructions:
1. Fold top and bottom edges to center.
2. Fold top and bottom edges to center a second time.
3. Pleat firmly from the left edge. Sharpen edges with hot iron.
4. Spread out fan. Balance flat folds of each side on table. Well-starched napkins will hold shape.

LILY

Effective and pretty on table.

Instructions:
1. Fold napkin into quarters.
2. Fold into triangle, closed corner to open points.
3. Turn two points over to other side. (Two points are on either side of closed point.)
4. Pleat.
5. Place closed end in glass. Pull down two points on each side and shape.

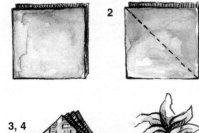

MEASUREMENTS & SUBSTITUTIONS

MEASUREMENTS

a pinch	1/8 teaspoon or less
3 teaspoons	1 tablespoon
4 tablespoons	1/4 cup
8 tablespoons	1/2 cup
12 tablespoons	3/4 cup
16 tablespoons	1 cup
2 cups	1 pint
4 cups	1 quart
4 quarts	1 gallon
8 quarts	1 peck
4 pecks	1 bushel
16 ounces	1 pound
32 ounces	1 quart
1 ounce liquid	2 tablespoons
8 ounces liquid	1 cup

Use standard measuring spoons and cups. All measurements are level.

C° TO F° CONVERSION

120° C	250° F
140° C	275° F
150° C	300° F
160° C	325° F
180° C	350° F
190° C	375° F
200° C	400° F
220° C	425° F
230° C	450° F

Temperature conversions are estimates.

SUBSTITUTIONS

Ingredient	Quantity	Substitute
baking powder	1 teaspoon	1/4 tsp. baking soda plus 1/2 tsp. cream of tartar
chocolate	1 square (1 oz.)	3 or 4 T. cocoa plus 1 T. butter
cornstarch	1 tablespoon	2 T. flour or 2 tsp. quick-cooking tapioca
cracker crumbs	3/4 cup	1 c. bread crumbs
dates	1 lb.	1 1/2 c. dates, pitted and cut
dry mustard	1 teaspoon	1 T. prepared mustard
flour, self-rising	1 cup	1 c. all-purpose flour, 1/2 tsp. salt, and 1 tsp. baking powder
herbs, fresh	1 tablespoon	1 tsp. dried herbs
ketchup or chili sauce	1 cup	1 c. tomato sauce plus 1/2 c. sugar and 2 T. vinegar (for use in cooking)
milk, sour	1 cup	1 T. lemon juice or vinegar plus sweet milk to make 1 c. (let stand 5 minutes)
whole	1 cup	1/2 c. evaporated milk plus 1/2 c. water
min. marshmallows	10	1 lg. marshmallow
onion, fresh	1 small	1 T. instant minced onion, rehydrated
sugar, brown	1/2 cup	2 T. molasses in 1/2 c. granulated sugar
powdered	1 cup	1 c. granulated sugar plus 1 tsp. cornstarch
tomato juice	1 cup	1/2 c. tomato sauce plus 1/2 c. water

When substituting cocoa for chocolate in cakes, the amount of flour must be reduced. Brown and white sugars usually can be interchanged.

SUGAR

EQUIVALENCY CHART

Food	Quantity	Yield
apple	1 medium	1 cup
banana, mashed	1 medium	1/3 cup
bread	1 1/2 slices	1 cup soft crumbs
bread	1 slice	1/4 cup fine, dry crumbs
butter	1 stick or 1/4 pound	1/2 cup
cheese, American, cubed	1 pound	2 2/3 cups
American, grated	1 pound	5 cups
cream cheese	3-ounce package	6 2/3 tablespoons
chocolate, bitter	1 square	1 ounce
cocoa	1 pound	4 cups
coconut	1 1/2 pound package	2 2/3 cups
coffee, ground	1 pound	5 cups
cornmeal	1 pound	3 cups
cornstarch	1 pound	3 cups
crackers, graham	14 squares	1 cup fine crumbs
saltine	28 crackers	1 cup fine crumbs
egg	4-5 whole	1 cup
whites	8-10	1 cup
yolks	10-12	1 cup
evaporated milk	1 cup	3 cups whipped
flour, cake, sifted	1 pound	4 1/2 cups
rye	1 pound	5 cups
white, sifted	1 pound	4 cups
white, unsifted	1 pound	3 3/4 cups
gelatin, flavored	3 1/4 ounces	1/2 cup
unflavored	1/4 ounce	1 tablespoon
lemon	1 medium	3 tablespoon juice
marshmallows	16	1/4 pound
noodles, cooked	8-ounce package	7 cups
uncooked	4 ounces (1 1/2 cups)	2-3 cups cooked
macaroni, cooked	8-ounce package	6 cups
macaroni, uncooked	4 ounces (1 1/4 cups)	2 1/4 cups cooked
spaghetti, uncooked	7 ounces	4 cups cooked
nuts, chopped	1/4 pound	1 cup
almonds	1 pound	3 1/2 cups
walnuts, broken	1 pound	3 cups
walnuts, unshelled	1 pound	1 1/2 to 1 3/4 cups
onion	1 medium	1/2 cup
orange	3-4 medium	1 cup juice
raisins	1 pound	3 1/2 cups
rice, brown	1 cup	4 cups cooked
converted	1 cup	3 1/2 cups cooked
regular	1 cup	3 cups cooked
wild	1 cup	4 cups cooked
sugar, brown	1 pound	2 1/2 cups
powdered	1 pound	3 1/2 cups
white	1 pound	2 cups
vanilla wafers	22	1 cup fine crumbs
zwieback, crumbled	4	1 cups

FOOD QUANTITIES

FOR LARGE SERVINGS

	25 Servings	50 Servings	100 Servings
Beverages:			
coffee	½ pound and 1 ½ gallons water	1 pound and 3 gallons water	2 pounds and 6 gallons water
lemonade	10-15 lemons and 1 ½ gallons water	20-30 lemons and 3 gallons water	40-60 lemons and 6 gallons water
tea	¹⁄₁₂ pound and 1 ½ gallons water	⅙ pound and 3 gallons water	⅓ pound and 6 gallons water
Desserts:			
layered cake	1 12" cake	3 10" cakes	6 10" cakes
sheet cake	1 10" x 12" cake	1 12" x 20" cake	2 12" x 20" cakes
watermelon	37 ½ pounds	75 pounds	150 pounds
whipping cream	¾ pint	1 ½ to 2 pints	3-4 pints
Ice cream:			
brick	3 ¼ quarts	6 ½ quarts	13 quarts
bulk	2 ¼ quarts	4 ½ quarts or 1 ¼ gallons	9 quarts or 2 ½ gallons
Meat, poultry or fish:			
fish	13 pounds	25 pounds	50 pounds
fish, fillets or steak	7 ½ pounds	15 pounds	30 pounds
hamburger	9 pounds	18 pounds	35 pounds
turkey or chicken	13 pounds	25 to 35 pounds	50 to 75 pounds
wieners (beef)	6 ½ pounds	13 pounds	25 pounds
Salads, casseroles:			
baked beans	¾ gallon	1 ¼ gallons	2 ½ gallons
jello salad	¾ gallon	1 ¼ gallons	2 ½ gallons
potato salad	4 ¼ quarts	2 ¼ gallons	4 ½ gallons
scalloped potatoes	4 ½ quarts or 1 12" x 20" pan	9 quarts or 2 ¼ gallons	18 quarts 4 ½ gallons
spaghetti	1 ¼ gallons	2 ½ gallons	5 gallons
Sandwiches:			
bread	50 slices or 3 1-pound loaves	100 slices or 6 1-pound loaves	200 slices or 12 1-pound loaves
butter	½ pound	1 pound	2 pounds
lettuce	1 ½ heads	3 heads	6 heads
mayonnaise	1 cup	2 cups	4 cups
mixed filling			
meat, eggs, fish	1 ½ quarts	3 quarts	6 quarts
jam, jelly	1 quart	2 quarts	4 quarts

QUICK FIXES

PRACTICALLY EVERYONE has experienced that dreadful moment in the kitchen when a recipe failed and dinner guests have arrived. Perhaps a failed timer, distraction or a missing or mismeasured ingredient is to blame. These handy tips can save the day!

Acidic foods – Sometimes a tomato-based sauce will become too acidic. Add baking soda, one teaspoon at a time, to the sauce. Use sugar as a sweeter alternative.

Burnt food on pots and pans – Allow the pan to cool on its own. Remove as much of the food as possible. Fill with hot water and add a capful of liquid fabric softener to the pot; let it stand for a few hours. You'll have an easier time removing the burnt food.

Chocolate seizes – Chocolate can seize (turn course and grainy) when it comes into contact with water. Place seized chocolate in a metal bowl over a large saucepan with an inch of simmering water in it. Over medium heat, slowly whisk in warm heavy cream. Use 1/4 cup cream to 4 ounces of chocolate. The chocolate will melt and become smooth.

Forgot to thaw whipped topping – Thaw in microwave for 1 minute on the defrost setting. Stir to blend well. Do not over thaw!

Hands smell like garlic or onion – Rinse hands under cold water while rubbing them with a large stainless steel spoon.

Hard brown sugar – Place in a paper bag and microwave for a few seconds, or place hard chunks in a food processor.

Jello too hard – Heat on a low microwave power setting for a very short time.

Lumpy gravy or sauce – Use a blender, food processor or simply strain.

No tomato juice – Mix 1/2 cup ketchup with 1/2 cup water.

Out of honey – Substitute 1 1/4 cups sugar dissolved in 1 cup water.

Overcooked sweet potatoes or carrots – Softened sweet potatoes and carrots make a wonderful soufflé with the addition of eggs and sugar. Consult your favorite cookbook for a good soufflé recipe. Overcooked sweet potatoes can also be used as pie filling.

Sandwich bread is stale – Toast or microwave bread briefly. Otherwise, turn it into breadcrumbs. Bread exposed to light and heat will hasten its demise, so consider using a bread box.

Soup, sauce, gravy too thin – Add 1 tablespoon of flour to hot soup, sauce or gravy. Whisk well (to avoid lumps) while the mixture is boiling. Repeat if necessary.

Sticky rice – Rinse rice with warm water.

Stew or soup is greasy – Refrigerate and remove grease once it congeals. Another trick is to lay cold lettuce leaves over the hot stew for about 10 seconds and then remove. Repeat as necessary.

Too salty – Add a little sugar and vinegar. For soups or sauces, add a raw peeled potato.

Too sweet – Add a little vinegar or lemon juice.

Undercooked cakes and cookies – Serve over vanilla ice cream. You can also layer pieces of cake or cookies with whipped cream and fresh fruit to form a dessert parfait. Crumbled cookies also make an excellent ice cream or cream pie topping.

COUNTING CALORIES

BEVERAGES

apple juice, 6 oz. 90
coffee (black) 0
cola, 12 oz. 115
cranberry juice, 6 oz. 115
ginger ale, 12 oz. 115
grape juice, (prepared from
   frozen concentrate), 6 oz. 142
lemonade, (prepared from
   frozen concentrate), 6 oz. 85
milk, protein fortified, 1 c. 105
   skim, 1 c. 90
   whole, 1 c. 160
orange juice, 6 oz. 85
pineapple juice, unsweetened, 6 oz. 95
root beer, 12 oz. 150
tonic (quinine water) 12 oz. 132

BREADS

cornbread, 1 sm. square 130
dumplings, 1 med. 70
French toast, 1 slice 135
melba toast, 1 slice 25
muffins, blueberry, 1 muffin 110
   bran, 1 muffin...................................106
   corn, 1 muffin...................................125
   English, 1 muffin 280
pancakes, 1 (4-in.) 60
pumpernickel, 1 slice 75
rye, 1 slice 60
waffle, 1 216
white, 1 slice 60-70
whole wheat, 1 slice 55-65

CEREALS

cornflakes, 1 c. 105
cream of wheat, 1 c. 120
oatmeal, 1 c. 148
rice flakes, 1 c. 105
shredded wheat, 1 biscuit 100
sugar krisps, 3/4 c. 110

CRACKERS

graham, 1 cracker 15-30
rye crisp, 1 cracker.............................35
saltine, 1 cracker.............................17-20
wheat thins, 1 cracker 9

DAIRY PRODUCTS

butter or margarine, 1 T. 100
cheese, American, 1 oz. 100
   camembert, 1 oz. 85
   cheddar, 1 oz. 115
   cottage cheese, 1 oz. 30
   mozzarella, 1 oz. 90
   parmesan, 1 oz. 130
   ricotta, 1 oz. 50
   roquefort, 1 oz. 105
   Swiss, 1 oz. 105
cream, light, 1 T. 30
   heavy, 1 T. 55
   sour, 1 T. 45
hot chocolate, with milk, 1 c. 277
milk chocolate, 1 oz. 145-155
yogurt
   made w/ whole milk, 1 c. 150-165
   made w/ skimmed milk, 1 c. 125

EGGS

fried, 1 lg. 100
poached or boiled, 1 lg. 75-80
scrambled or in omelet, 1 lg. 110-130

FISH AND SEAFOOD

bass, 4 oz. 105
salmon, broiled or baked, 3 oz. 155
sardines, canned in oil, 3 oz. 170
trout, fried, 3 1/2 oz. 220
tuna, in oil, 3 oz. 170
   in water, 3 oz. 110

COUNTING CALORIES

FRUITS

apple, 1 med. 80-100
applesauce, sweetened, 1/2 c. 90-115
    unsweetened, 1/2 c. 50
banana, 1 med. 85
blueberries, 1/2 c. 45
cantaloupe, 1/2 c. 24
cherries (pitted), raw, 1/2 c. 40
grapefruit, 1/2 med. 55
grapes, 1/2 c. 35-55
honeydew, 1/2 c. 55
mango, 1 med. 90
orange, 1 med. 65-75
peach, 1 med. 35
pear, 1 med. 60-100
pineapple, fresh, 1/2 c. 40
    canned in syrup, 1/2 c. 95
plum, 1 med. 30
strawberries, fresh, 1/2 c. 30
    frozen and sweetened, 1/2 c. ..120-140
tangerine, 1 lg. 39
watermelon, 1/2 c. 42

MEAT AND POULTRY

beef, ground (lean), 3 oz. 185
    roast, 3 oz. 185
chicken, broiled, 3 oz. 115
lamb chop (lean), 3 oz. 175-200
steak, sirloin, 3 oz. 175
    tenderloin, 3 oz. 174
    top round, 3 oz. 162
turkey, dark meat, 3 oz. 175
    white meat, 3 oz. 150
veal, cutlet, 3 oz. 156
    roast, 3 oz. 76

NUTS

almonds, 2 T. 105
cashews, 2 T. 100
peanuts, 2 T. 105
peanut butter, 1 T. 95
pecans, 2 T. 95
pistachios, 2 T. 92
walnuts, 2 T. 80

PASTA

macaroni or spaghetti,
    cooked, 3/4 c. 115

SALAD DRESSINGS

blue cheese, 1 T. 70
French, 1 T. 65
Italian, 1 T. 80
mayonnaise, 1 T. 100
olive oil, 1 T. 124
Russian, 1 T. 70
salad oil, 1 T. 120

SOUPS

bean, 1 c. 130-180
beef noodle, 1 c. 70
bouillon and consomme, 1 c. 30
chicken noodle, 1 c. 65
chicken with rice, 1 c. 50
minestrone, 1 c. 80-150
split pea, 1 c. 145-170
tomato with milk, 1 c. 170
vegetable, 1 c. 80-100

VEGETABLES

asparagus, 1 c. 35
broccoli, cooked, 1/2 c. 25
cabbage, cooked, 1/2 c. 15-20
carrots, cooked, 1/2 c. 25-30
cauliflower, 1/2 c. 10-15
corn (kernels), 1/2 c. 70
green beans, 1 c. 30
lettuce, shredded, 1/2 c. 5
mushrooms, canned, 1/2 c. 20
onions, cooked, 1/2 c. 30
peas, cooked, 1/2 c. 60
potato, baked, 1 med. 90
    chips, 8-10 100
    mashed, w/milk & butter, 1 c. ..200-300
spinach, 1 c. 40
tomato, raw, 1 med. 25
    cooked, 1/2 c. 30

COOKING TERMS

Au gratin: Topped with crumbs and/or cheese and browned in oven or under broiler.

Au jus: Served in its own juices.

Baste: To moisten foods during cooking with pan drippings or special sauce in order to add flavor and prevent drying.

Bisque: A thick cream soup.

Blanch: To immerse in rapidly boiling water and allow to cook slightly.

Cream: To soften a fat, especially butter, by beating it at room temperature. Butter and sugar are often creamed together, making a smooth, soft paste.

Crimp: To seal the edges of a two-crust pie either by pinching them at intervals with the fingers or by pressing them together with the tines of a fork.

Crudites: An assortment of raw vegetables (i.e. carrots, broccoli, celery, mushrooms) that is served as an hors d'oeuvre, often accompanied by a dip.

Degrease: To remove fat from the surface of stews, soups or stock. Usually cooled in the refrigerator so that fat hardens and is easily removed.

Dredge: To coat lightly with flour, cornmeal, etc.

Entree: The main course.

Fold: To incorporate a delicate substance, such as whipped cream or beaten egg whites, into another substance without releasing air bubbles. A spatula is used to gently bring part of the mixture from the bottom of the bowl to the top. The process is repeated, while slowly rotating the bowl, until the ingredients are thoroughly blended.

Glaze: To cover with a glossy coating, such as a melted and somewhat diluted jelly for fruit desserts.

Julienne: To cut or slice vegetables, fruits or cheeses into match-shaped slivers.

Marinate: To allow food to stand in a liquid in order to tenderize or to add flavor.

Meuniére: Dredged with flour and sautéed in butter.

Mince: To chop food into very small pieces.

Parboil: To boil until partially cooked; to blanch. Usually final cooking in a seasoned sauce follows this procedure.

Pare: To remove the outermost skin of a fruit or vegetable.

Poach: To cook gently in hot liquid kept just below the boiling point.

Purée: To mash foods by hand by rubbing through a sieve or food mill, or by whirling in a blender or food processor until perfectly smooth.

Refresh: To run cold water over food that has been parboiled in order to stop the cooking process quickly.

Sauté: To cook and/or brown food in a small quantity of hot shortening.

Scald: To heat to just below the boiling point, when tiny bubbles appear at the edge of the saucepan.

Simmer: To cook in liquid just below the boiling point. The surface of the liquid should be barely moving, broken from time to time by slowly rising bubbles.

Steep: To let food stand in hot liquid in order to extract or to enhance flavor, like tea in hot water or poached fruit in syrup.

Toss: To combine ingredients with a repeated lifting motion.

Whip: To beat rapidly in order to incorporate air and produce expansion, as in heavy cream or egg whites.

Welcome to...

BOB KERBY'S
LONGHORN STUDIO

Share in the spirit
of the American West!

Dear Friends,

We wish to invite you to experience the West through the beautiful creations of artist Bob Kerby. Please find below a brief description of Bob's most popular products as well as some fantastic opportunities to raise money for your club and/or yourself.

To receive our full color brochure and learn more about Kerby art, simply mark the products of interest on the card enclosed.

We look forward to hearing from you!

Sincerely,

Kerby's Longhorn Studio

P.S. Be sure to visit our website at www.ExperienceTheWest.com

Bob Kerby Art Creations...

* Bob's exclusive, deluxe **Range Riders Appointment Calendar** features 12 beautiful full-color paintings. There is also ample room to record your daily appointments. We will also personalize the calandars for your business. Great Christmas gifts for your friends and customers! (size 11" x 18")

* You'll enjoy our **Range Riders Note & Christmas Cards**. Share your warmest wishes with friends and loved ones. Each full color Christmas card features a beautiful Kerby snow scene (size 5"x7") with matching blue envelopes.

* Our Print Gallery includes a gorgeous collection of **limited and open edition collector prints.** Now you can create that special western feel you've always wanted for your home or office. We also have just the print to be shared as a special gift for the western enthusiasts in your life!

* If you are looking for a high-quality piece, you will treasure **original Kerby oil pantings.** Each one-of-a-kind piece is beautifully framed. Many hang in public and private collections nationwide.

* Now you can earn extra money by having a **Range Riders Gift Party** in your home or on-line. Invite your friends. Let us show you how it works. It's fun and easy!

* If you need to **raise money** for your club or organization, we have a no risk program that produces results. We'll provide everything you'll need. This is a real unique opportunity to raise money for trips, special projects, a new acquisition, or for any worthy cause. It's simple and lucrative!